INTARSIA
WOODWORKING FOR BEGINNERS

Sunflower, page 88.

INTARSIA

WOODWORKING FOR BEGINNERS

SKILL-BUILDING LESSONS FOR CREATING BEAUTIFUL WOOD MOSAICS

BY KATHY WISE

FOX CHAPEL
PUBLISHING

Intarsia Woodworking for Beginners is an original work, first published in 2009 by Fox Chapel Publishing Company, Inc. The patterns contained herein are copyrighted by the author. Readers may make copies of these patterns for personal use. The patterns themselves, however, are not to be duplicated for resale or distribution under any circumstances. Any such copying is a violation of copyright law.

ISBN 978-1-56523-442-0

Library of Congress Cataloging-in-Publication Data

Wise, Kathy.

Intarsia woodworking for beginners / by Kathy Wise.

    p. cm.

Includes index.

ISBN: 978-1-56523-442-0

1. Marquetry. 2. Woodwork--Patterns. I. Title.
TT192.W56 2009
745.51'2--dc22

                             2009025324

To learn more about the other great books from Fox Chapel Publishing, or to find a retailer near you, call toll-free 800-457-9112 or visit us at *www.FoxChapelPublishing.com*.

Note to Authors: We are always looking for talented authors to write new books in our area of woodworking, design, and related crafts. Please send a brief letter describing your idea to Acquisition Editor, 1970 Broad Street, East Petersburg, PA 17520.

Printed in China
First printing: November 2009

CONTENTS

About the Author

Although Kathy Wise was a city girl for most of her childhood, she always had a strong love for animals. When she was a teenager, her family moved to a rural area in the thumb area of Michigan. She fell in love with country living almost instantly.

Kathy credits her mother, who is also an artist, for her interest in art. As a child, Kathy busily sculpted animals from soap and wood while her mother painted landscapes and people. High school and college art classes intensified her interest in art and sculpture. Adding sculpted clay animal figures to her pots during a ceramics class in college led to the creation of many other animal sculptures. Students were soon asking Kathy to create animals for them. Kathy

Kathy Wise shown with her lifesize intarsia project, Baby Giraffe—705 pieces, 6' x 26" (1829mm x 660mm).

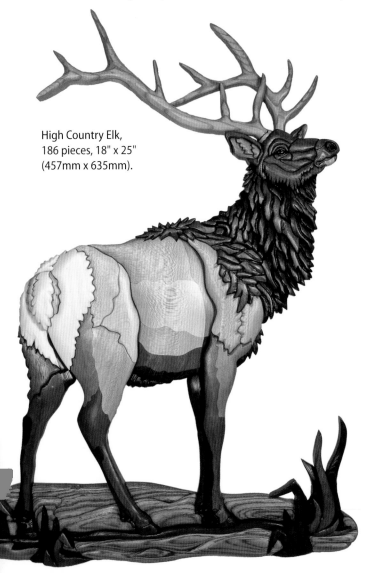

High Country Elk, 186 pieces, 18" x 25" (457mm x 635mm).

graduated Magna Cum Laude with an Associates Degree in Commercial Art.

Kathy began selling her one-of-a-kind animal sculptures at art fairs and shows. Soon she was supplying over 70 stores nationwide. In 1983, Gene Freedman (then president of Enesco Corporation) first saw Kathy's work in a Seattle gift shop. This man, who launched Precious Moments, saw potential in Kathy's art and contacted her to start the first of her many lines in the giftware industry. She has gone on to design animal figures and giftware for many other companies, including Simson, Westland, United Design, and Encore Group. Over the years, Kathy has designed and sculpted over one thousand different items in over forty lines that have been sold worldwide.

Kathy first began designing intarsia patterns for her father-in-law, Phil MacDonald. When his customers would ask for a special dog breed or custom intarsia of their pet, he would ask Kathy to create the pattern. She started to market the patterns and found intarsia artists loved her designs. She offers the greatest variety of dog breed intarsia patterns found anywhere. With Kathy's knowledge and background in sculpting dogs, each pattern has a unique personality that is not found in any other intarsia patterns available in the marketplace.

In fall of 2004, *Scroll Saw Woodworking & Crafts* published Kathy's first article, which featured her Boston terrier intarsia design and step-by-step instructions. Over 20 articles followed, including a bird wreath, calico cat, Arabian horse, maple leaf picture frame, turkey, and other assorted wildlife. Kathy's art has been featured on several *SSW&C* covers. Her first book, *Intarsia Woodworking Projects*, features 21 projects ranging from beginner to advanced skill level. Kathy works on new patterns, articles, and beginner kits. She accepts special commissions for her intarsia work, including murals and large wall pieces. Her intarsia pieces are signed limited editions.

Go to Kathy Wise Designs for all of your intarsia pattern needs. Dog breeds, cats, horses, wildlife, landscapes, and more are available. For a free catalog of over 400 intarsia patterns, contact:

Kathy Wise Designs Inc.
PO Box 60
Yale, MI 48097
www.kathywise.com
kathywise@bignet.net
Fax: 810-387-9044

Tiger Trail, 1045 pieces, 42" x 30" (1067mm x 762mm)—1st place winner in the intarsia category at the highly acclaimed 2009 Design in Wood Show in Del Mar, California.

Labrador-ables, 288 pieces, 34" x 19" (864mm x 483mm).

Introduction

Intarsia is an early Italian process of inlaying various colored woods onto a wood background. Over the years, it has evolved into a more sculptural style of wood-crafted art. Each intarsia artist (intarsianist) has his or her own technique and approach to the art form. I firmly believe there is no right or wrong way to create intarsia, just different intarsia styles. I like to use natural woods as much as possible in my work, but I use some stains or paints if I think it will add to the finished work. Having been a sculptor of animals and dogs for over 30 years, I like to add as much 3-D effect to my intarsia art as possible. The color of the wood in an intarsia piece is very important, as well as the light and dark values used in the design.

Subject matter often determines whether the piece will be viewed as a craft item or as a piece of art. Realistic animals and landscapes done in natural wood tones will be more accepted as art then a cutie train stained bright colors, no matter how nicely done it is. I have included a variety of intarsia patterns in this book, both fun and realistic designs.

This book will cover the basic skills needed to introduce you to the wonderful art of intarsia. If you are a beginner, follow the skill-building lessons in order; each project builds on the previous lessons. If you are already skilled in creating intarsia, browse through the lessons and projects—you will find many helpful hints and shortcuts. Feel free to change the patterns, substitute exotic woods, or add other materials, such as glass, stone, or plastic. Use stains, paints, oils, or dyes to enhance your colors to achieve the look you want. Add as much depth as possible to your intarsia piece to make it jump out at you. The pattern is just a starting point and guide for your own special brand of artistic creativity; make these projects into your own personal masterpieces of intarsia art. Above all, have fun!

—Kathy Wise

How to Use This Book

This book is structured so anyone—even someone without any knowledge of intarsia—can create beautiful works of art. The lessons break down the important techniques and steps of intarsia so they are easily understood. If you have never worked with a scroll saw or are not yet comfortable cutting basic lines, go to the appendix on page 114 for simple cutting exercises.

Chapter 1 introduces the concepts of intarsia through six simple lessons. When you complete your first intarsia piece—a goldfish—you will understand the basics of working with an intarsia pattern, cutting, sanding, gluing, creating a backer board, and finishing.

Chapter 2 explains how to turn multiple pieces of wood into a colorful intarsia butterfly. Lessons 7 through 10 describe the nuances of working with multiple wood shades—understanding the patterns, cutting, creating color breaks, and fitting the pieces together.

Chapter 3 teaches a few techniques that will take your beginner intarsia to the next level. Lessons 11 through 17 illuminate the topics of stains, shims, overlays, laminations, woodburning, and carving texture.

Chapter 4 contains a wealth of projects for you to create. The 20 projects are divided into three levels. Each grouping starts off with a detailed step-by-step project. The rest of the pieces show everything you need to recreate the intarsia shown: a pattern, reference photos, materials list, and even helpful tips and hints.

The **Level 1** section of Chapter 4 contains the Iris Step-by-Step, as well as a beagle, tortoise, panda, and several photo frame projects.

Level 2 starts off with the elegant Horse Step-by-Step project. Following are a selection of wonderful projects, including a sunflower, frog, and lighthouse.

The **Level 3** section contains the most difficult projects in this book. After creating the step-by-step project, Girl with Boots, you can graduate to a handful of beautiful pieces worth the effort. They include a cross, raccoon, and birdfeeder.

The **Appendix** contains extra practice exercises and simple patterns to help you refine your cutting and fitting techniques.

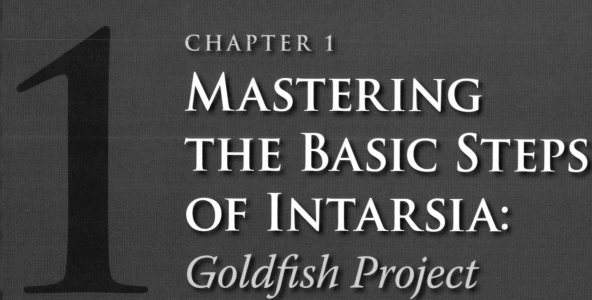

CHAPTER 1

MASTERING THE BASIC STEPS OF INTARSIA:
Goldfish Project

This chapter utilizes photo-packed lessons to teach

you the basic steps of intarsia—from how to work

with a simple pattern all the way through to attaching

the hanger. You will construct the 11-piece goldfish

project by following along with the lessons. To help

you learn the basic steps, only one type of wood is

used for this piece. I chose a piece of yellowheart for a

nice bright yellow. If you are just learning to cut, use a

softer wood, such as poplar or cedar—it will be easier

to cut and shape. You can also stain or paint spots on

your goldfish for a variety of looks.

Goldfish

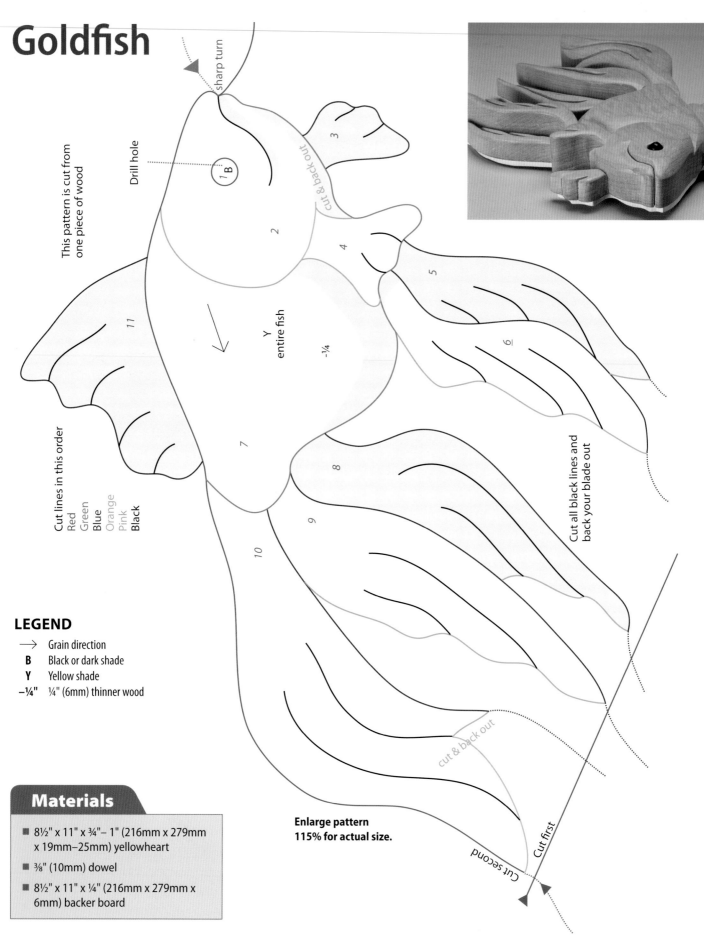

This pattern is cut from one piece of wood

sharp turn

Drill hole

1 B

2

3

cut & back out

4

5

11

Y
entire fish

–¼

6

7

8

9

10

Cut all black lines and back your blade out

Cut lines in this order
Red
Green
Blue
Orange
Pink
Black

cut & back out

LEGEND

→   Grain direction

B   Black or dark shade

Y   Yellow shade

–¼"   ¼" (6mm) thinner wood

**Enlarge pattern
115% for actual size.**

Cut first

Cut second

Materials

- 8½" x 11" x ¾"– 1" (216mm x 279mm x 19mm–25mm) yellowheart
- ⅜" (10mm) dowel
- 8½" x 11" x ¼" (216mm x 279mm x 6mm) backer board

LESSON 1:

Understanding and Working with Simple Intarsia Patterns

Intarsia patterns have a good bit of information on them—wood color suggestions, grain direction arrows, shaded grey shaping areas, shim lines, and woodburning lines, for starters. Another thing to consider is how many copies of the pattern you need. After you read this lesson, you will have a better understanding of how to work with and use intarsia patterns.

Symbols: Look over the pattern on page 12.

Notice the **grain direction arrows**. They are suggestions, so if you find a piece of wood that looks good because of its grain pattern, disregard the arrows.

Positive and negative fractions refer to the level of the piece that is either greater or lesser than the rest of the project. A negative number means using thinner wood or sanding down; a positive number means you need to cut a shim or use thicker wood to raise the piece to that level.

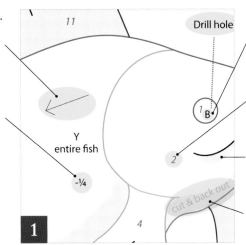

The **letters** correspond with the legend to tell you what color wood is recommended for each piece.

Numbers are included to identify each piece. This number will be transferred to the back of each cut piece to help you remember where it goes.

Gray shaded shaping areas are shaping guides that help you to know what areas are to be sanded lower.

Additional instructions can also appear on patterns.

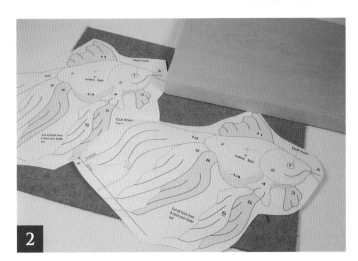

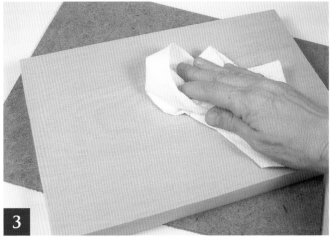

Copy: Make 3 copies of your pattern: one to keep as a spare, one to cut the fish, and one to use on your backer board. Cut out the patterns. I recommend making the spare copy because if I happen to need one in the middle of the process, I won't have to stop what I'm doing to go make copies.

Clean: Be sure to wipe your board clean of dust and dirt before attaching the pattern to the wood. If your board is not flat, plane or sand it. Uneven or warped boards will make your cutting and fitting difficult.

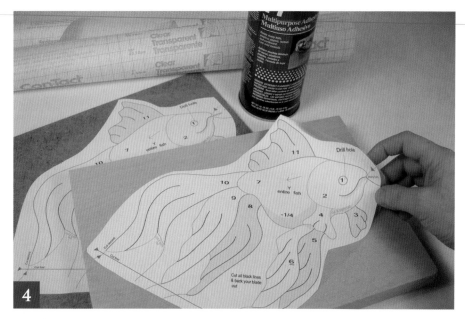

Attach: Spray the back of your patterns with spray adhesive and stick to the shiny side of clear contact paper. Then cut out your patterns and peel the paper backing off. Stick to your wood, lining up your grain direction arrows.

Checkpoint: Here is what the project looks like at this point.

Tips

- The pattern attached to the backer board can be used as a work surface. Later you will trace your outline on top of the pattern and cut it out, allowing for any adjustments.

- If you are using Masonite as a backer board, be sure to attach your pattern to the rough side of the board.

- Trim down your goldfish board if needed to make it easier to handle while cutting.

- Using spray adhesive with contact paper will make it easy to remove the pattern pieces and reposition if you choose. It also will not leave a sticky residue on the wood.

LESSON 2:
Cutting Simple Intarsia

Beginners are often at a loss where to begin to cut. By cutting certain lines in a project, you can open up your project and make later cuts easier. As you cut more projects, you will know which lines to start with at a glance. With this in mind, the goldfish pattern is color-coded to make it easier for beginners. If you don't have access to a color copier, keep the book handy to refer back to for the correct cutting order.

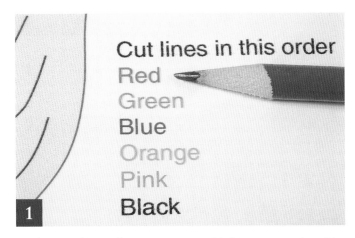

Review cutting order: Make sure your blade is square to the table and your wood is flat. Use a #5 reverse tooth blade or the blade of your choice to cut the lines in order of the colors, starting with the red lines. As you cut each line in order, it will open up the pieces, making the next lines easier to cut.

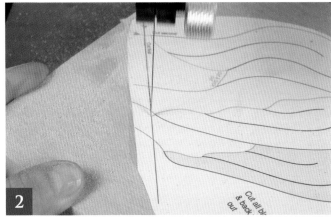

Cut straight lines: This pattern is all curves, but you can start with a straight line across the tip of the fins to get rid of some of the waste material. Cut slowly and push from the front, not the sides, as you cut. Let the blade do the cutting. Many beginners are impatient and push too fast when first starting to cut, which results in bowed cuts, poor fitting, and broken blades.

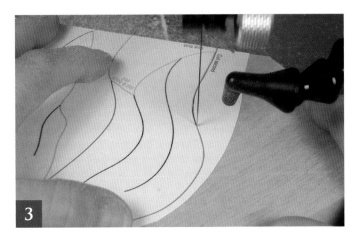

Cut curves: Cut the red line on top of the fish. Turn your wood slowly as you push forward to cut along the curves. Keep the blade on the line. If your blade does wander off, ease it back on to the line. You are cutting one piece of wood, so your pieces will fit even if you wander off the lines.

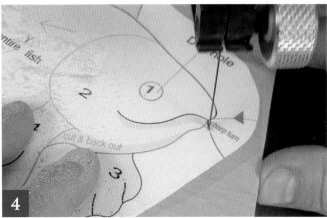

Cut sharp angles: When you get to the sharp turn at the lip, stop moving your wood, cease pushing, and let the blade stay running in place. Twist your wood as you put slight backward pressure on the blade. This turns the blade in the area already cut without taking more wood from the front. After you turn it to the correct position, push the wood into the blade to finish your turn. Smaller blades make sharp turns easier.

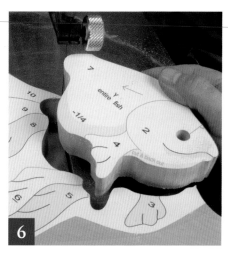

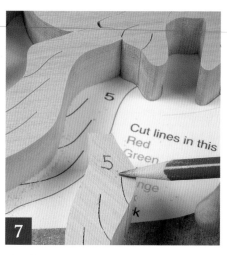

5

Drill entry holes: Blade entry holes are drilled when an interior piece must be cut out. It is a good idea to drill holes before your pieces are all cut out and the piece becomes too small to handle. Using a bit larger than the size of your saw blade, drill a hole in the eye section. Sand the bottom to remove any burrs. Insert the blade and cut out the circle.

6

Free a piece: Cut the green and blue lines. Remove the pieces from the board. Continue cutting in the color order until all pieces are cut out. If a piece doesn't come out easily, try removing it from the other side. Cut and then back out your blade on all the black lines.

7

Number: Number each piece on its back in pencil. Peel off all of the paper patterns from the front of each piece.

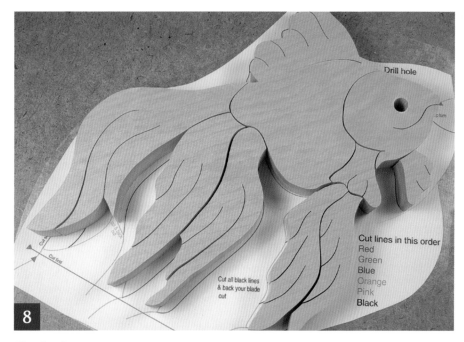

8

Checkpoint: Lay out all of your pieces in place on your backer board pattern.

Tips

- Cut larger pieces down to smaller, easier-to-handle sizes by cutting the lines that bisect the piece (see Step 6). Look for lines that don't have sharp curves or dead ends.

- Continue cutting a line straight off the edge of the wood if that will eliminate the need to make a sharp turn.

- Make turnaround loops for sharp exterior turns in the waste area only.

- Instead of doing the interior cut for the eye, you can use a ⅜" (10mm) bit and drill the hole to the size of the dowel.

- If a piece is hard to remove from the others, you may be pushing too hard on your wood, causing the blade to bow. This makes an uneven curved cut on the sides of your wood. Slow down and let the blade do its job.

LESSON 3:
How to Sand and Shape Intarsia Pieces

To give your project more depth and dimension, make the pieces that would be the farthest away from you thinner. An example of this would be the back fin of the goldfish (piece 3). I usually cut all of my pieces from the same thickness of wood, and then sand or cut down to the level indicated. Use the sanding guide and side photo of the project to help with sanding the levels.

Mark: Mark the areas that are lower, using the shaping guide on the pattern. Use the pattern and the reference photos of the project to decide how thin to sand the pieces. Sand the lowest (shaded) pieces first.

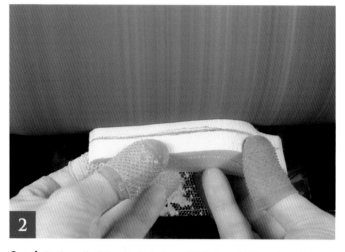

Sand: Gather all of the shaded pieces (3, 5, 8, and 11) and sand them so they appear much lower than the rest of the project. I sand these to ½" (13mm) thick with a drum sander. Hold your piece so you can see the marked line—sand to the mark and rotate to ensure all sides are sanded to the mark.

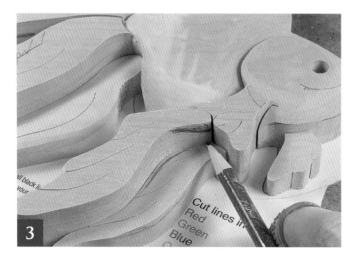

Check: Replace and remark your pieces often. It is better to sand your piece down a little bit at a time and recheck the levels frequently than to sand away too much and have to recut a piece. I replace my pieces several times until they are at the desired elevation. When the sanded pieces are close to the same height and make the project look dimensional, you've reached your goal.

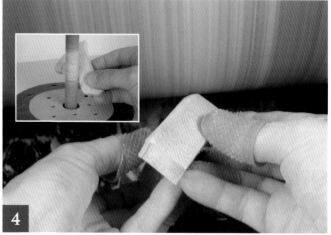

Round the edges: Round the edges of the highest pieces (2, 4, 6, 7, 9, and 10) slightly by pressing the edges against the drum sander at a 45° angle. Take about ¼" (6mm) at the very edges. For tighter inside curves, you will have to use a ½" (13mm) sanding band on a rotary tool. If you like, you can do a bit of hand or power carving to accent the lines on the fins and under the mouth.

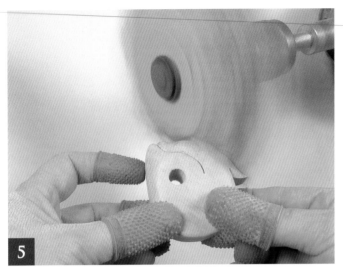

Use sanding mop: Use a sanding mop for a fast and easy way to finish sanding your pieces. Unless you like to hand sand, this is the best way to get a smooth surface on your pieces. If you can attach your mop to a grinder or drill press with variable speed, you will be able to control the RPM, which will prevent burn marks on some types of wood.

Make the eye: Round the tip of a ⅜" (10mm) dowel on the drum sander. Use the sanding mop to finish sanding the tip. Hold the eye in place and mark the bottom of the dowel. Cut on the scroll saw. Stain, paint, or burn black.

Checkpoint: Lay out all of your pieces on the work pattern and check to make sure you are satisfied with the sanded levels. Make sure the adjoining edges at the tail and the body flow into each other. The long fins (5 and 6) should be below the short fin (4).

Tips

- Use rubber fingertip covers to protect your fingers from the sander (available at office supply stores).

- Wear eye protection and a face mask.

- Have a good dust collection system in place. Many woods have toxic dust.

- Have a work table on rollers that you can move around your shop from saw to sander easily.

- Hand sand areas that are hard to get to. Using a nail emery board works well for small areas.

- Hold your pieces at an angle to the light to check for scratches and bumps and re-sand where needed.

- Don't be afraid of sanding. If you do remove too much wood and your piece is ruined, recut another piece and sand again. It is all a learning process.

- Lightly hold pieces to the edge of the mop—if you push them too hard into the mop, the pieces will be caught and hurled to the ground. If you are sanding small pieces, use pliers or forceps to hold the pieces.

LESSON 4:

How to Glue the Pieces Together

I use thick gap-filling CA glue to tack the pieces together before I glue them in one piece to the backer board. Accelerator speeds up setting time to about 5-10 seconds. If you use accelerator, spray it on one side of a piece before you put dots of CA on the other piece.

Caution! Cyanoacrylate (CA) glue can cause allergic skin reaction and is an eye and respiratory irritant. Use adequate ventilation any time you are using the glue, or are sanding or cutting areas that have been glued. Cutting along glued lines will heat up the glue and release fumes, so use a fan to blow the air away from your face.

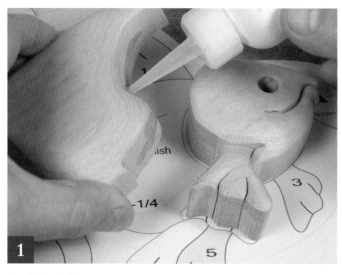

Apply CA glue: To begin gluing your goldfish together, apply a bead of CA glue to the body (7) and press the head (2) and fin (4) to it. Press into place and leave in place to set up for a few minutes. When dry, move on to the next few pieces and continue until all of the parts are glued together.

Using CA with accelerator

If you use the accelerator, you must be sure to put the pieces in the correct place quickly. Glue one piece at a time, adding pieces as you go. Spray the accelerator on one side of  a piece and put dots of CA on the other piece. Press and hold the pieces in place on a flat surface and twist slightly as it sets. Twisting stops the pieces from gluing to the paper and enables you to move quickly to add the next pieces. When dry, move on to the next few pieces and continue until all the parts are glued together. Go to page 45 for more information on CA gluing.

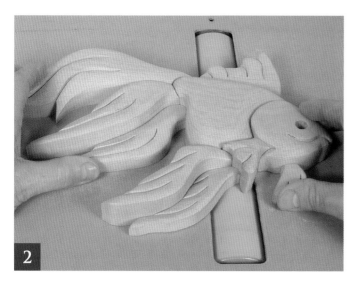

Sand the bottom: When you are done gluing, flat sand the bottom. This will create a nice flat surface to glue to the backer board. If you don't have a flat sander, be sure to clean off any paper or glue from the bottom.

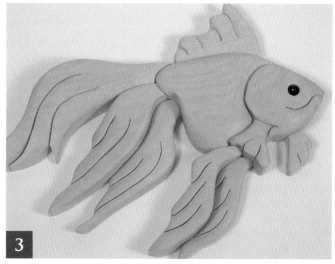

Checkpoint: Your goldfish is glued together and has a flat underside.

Using Silicone Glue: Flower Project

You will notice after putting a project together and laying it on top of your original pattern that it is often smaller. This is because of the kerf (wood removed from cutting the line). All the kerf lines add up, and as more pieces are cut, more gaps can appear. Silicone tacking is a wonderful solution for spacing out the gaps so they are not noticeable. Because it is thick and tacky, silicone fills spaces as well as sticking pieces together. It will also pull apart easily if you need to reposition pieces when you are gluing the sections to the backer board. If you use silicone instead of CA glue, your seams might not be as tight over the entire piece, but you will spend less time fitting and the results will be very good.

Use 100% silicone clear glue or caulk. You can buy it in a small tube at any hardware store. Put a small amount between each piece and put back in place on your pattern work board. Make sure you don't use too much or it will show through the cracks. Space each piece so the gap is gone. Let dry overnight.

Notice when you push the pieces tightly together that you have a gap at one side. If you were to CA glue this piece together the gap would remain.

With silicone, the gap disappears because it is spaced out between all the pieces.

Materials

- 7" x 7" x ¾" (178mm x 178mm x 19mm) medium-light wood (cedar)

Tips

- Always put the CA glue on the smallest piece and the accelerator on the other piece.

- Glue small pieces together as you work; they will be easier to handle.

- Round the center.

- Use silicone glue to attach the pieces together. The project will fit better and easier than if you use CA glue.

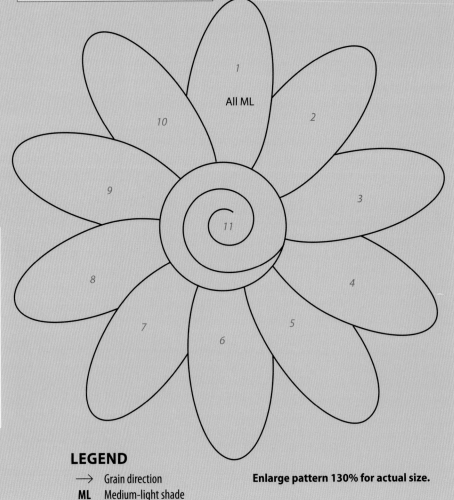

All ML

LEGEND

→   Grain direction
ML   Medium-light shade

Enlarge pattern 130% for actual size.

LESSON 5:
How to Create the Backer Board

A backer board is a piece of wood attached to the back of your project. It lends extra support—and a clean look—to the back of the intarsia project. Backer boards are cut after you have completed gluing the rest of your project. You can use Masonite, luan, or a good grade of plywood for your backer boards. The back of your project should look as good as the front—take pride in your workmanship.

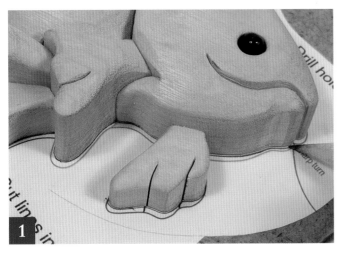

Trace: Lay the goldfish on top of the pattern stuck to the backer board. Using a sharp pencil, trace the outline. You will notice it is a bit smaller than the pattern, due to the kerf.

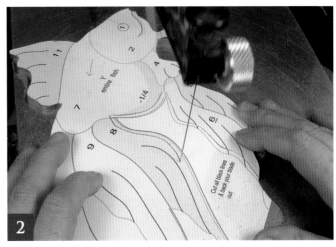

Cut: Use a #3 or #5 reverse tooth blade to cut a clean edge. Cut just inside the marked lines—about ⅛" (3mm). You want the edge of the board to be slightly inside the outline of the project.

Sand: Sand the edges of the backer board with the drum sander and/or sanding mop. You can also sand a bevel or cut on the edge, if desired.

Paint: Paint or stain the edges and back of the board as desired, unless you are using Masonite. Do not paint the glue side of the backer board, as your adhesive will not adhere well to the painted surface.

5

Glue: Put dots of wood glue and dots of CA glue on the back of your project, being sure to get some glue on every section. Spray the backer board with accelerator. Lay your project upside down on a soft cloth to prevent scratches. Hold your backer board over the project and press the pieces together. You will only have about 7-10 seconds before the CA sets up and acts as a clamp for the wood glue. You can move right on to the spray finish steps.

Gluing with wood glue

If you want to use wood glue instead of CA, you will have to clamp the project and the backer board together and let set overnight. You can use sand bags to put pressure on the pieces if you don't have clamps.

6

Checkpoint: Your project is now attached to a backer board.

Tips

- You don't have to use a pattern to cut the backer board—you can trace right on the backer wood.

- If using Masonite, be sure the rough side is up so the nice smooth finish will show on the back.

- Cut slightly inside the backer board line—you want the board to be smaller than the project.

- Sand or cut a bevel on the board edges for a clean effect.

LESSON 6:
How to Finish

The finish is the last step in your intarsia project: spraying the piece with a clear protective finish and installing a hanger to display your intarsia. Make test samples of varnishes on several different types of wood. This will let you see how the wood will look after it is finished. Keep an inventory of your samples for future reference.

Tips

- Make sure you don't apply the spray finish too heavily—it will run.

- Use a white gel varnish to keep white wood from yellowing when the varnish is applied.

- Use gel varnish for a beautiful and easy to apply finish.

- After the varnish is dry the grain may rise up, leaving a rough finish. Use a brown paper bag or very fine steel wool to rub the area.

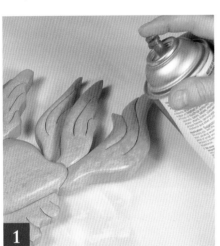

1

Spray: Make sure your project is free of dust. Spray your finish of choice using the manufacturer's directions. I like using clear satin polyurethane. Let dry completely between coats. Put a clear gloss on the eye for a realistic look.

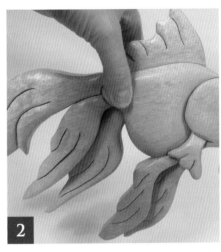

2

Balance point: Hold the goldfish in the middle between your thumb and forefinger to find the balance point. Move your fingers until the piece hangs level freely. Mark the spot.

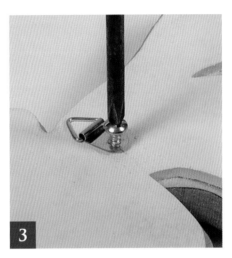

3

Drill: At the balance point, drill a hole for the screw to attach the hanger. Be sure not to drill all the way through to the front and ruin your piece. Screw in the mirror-style hanger.

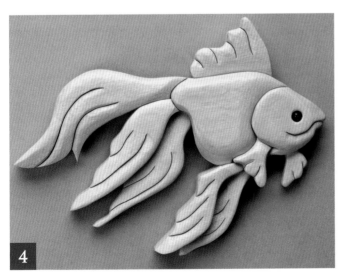

4

Checkpoint: You're done! The goldfish is now finished and complete with a hanger. Now that you see how easy intarsia can be, you are ready to move on to more precise cutting and fitting using different types and colors of wood.

Another fish in the sea

Another option for finishing is adding a light orange (or another color) acrylic wash on white wood for a brightly spotted goldfish. See Lesson 11 on page 36 for more information on stains and washes.

CHAPTER 2

SIMPLE MULTIPLE-WOOD INTARSIA:
Butterfly Project

This introduction to multiple-wood intarsia reviews

the basics you learned in Chapter 1. The lessons in this

chapter highlight the new steps you will use with the

addition of more than one color of wood. When you have

completed this 11-piece, three-color butterfly, you'll be

ready to move on to more complex intarsia projects.

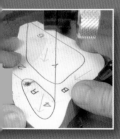

Butterfly

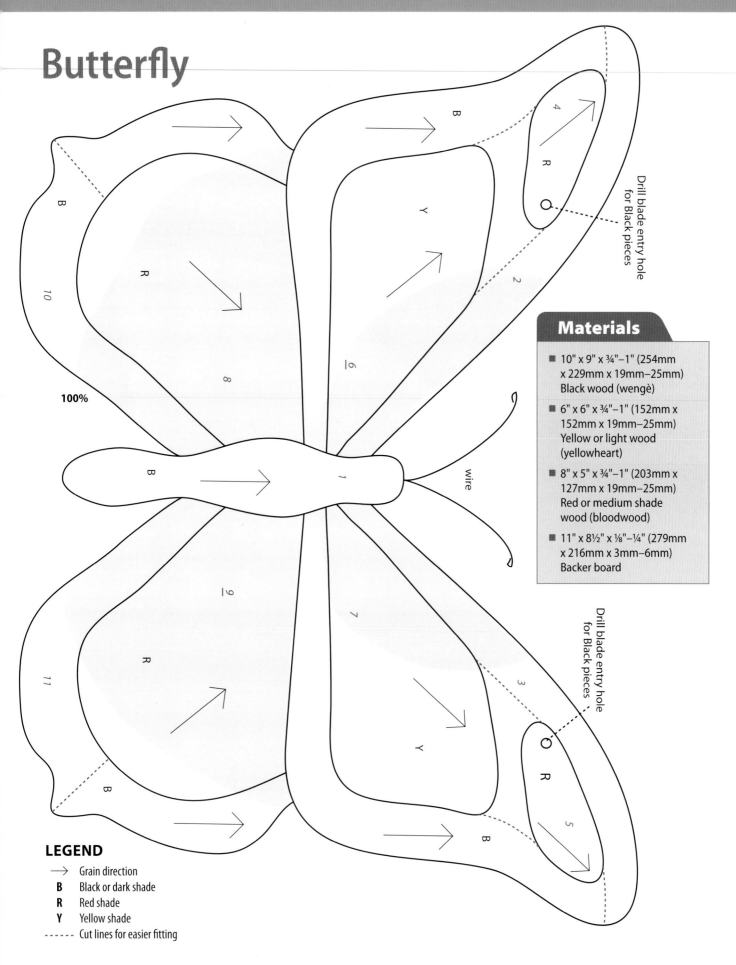

Drill blade entry hole for Black pieces

B

R

4

R

Y

2

B

10

R

8

6

100%

B

1

wire

9

7

Y

R

11

B

3

Drill blade entry hole for Black pieces

R

5

B

Materials

- 10" x 9" x ¾"–1" (254mm x 229mm x 19mm–25mm) Black wood (wengè)
- 6" x 6" x ¾"–1" (152mm x 152mm x 19mm–25mm) Yellow or light wood (yellowheart)
- 8" x 5" x ¾"–1" (203mm x 127mm x 19mm–25mm) Red or medium shade wood (bloodwood)
- 11" x 8½" x ⅛"–¼" (279mm x 216mm x 3mm–6mm) Backer board

LEGEND

→   Grain direction
B   Black or dark shade
R   Red shade
Y   Yellow shade
- - - -   Cut lines for easier fitting

LESSON 7:

Understanding and Working with Multiple-Color Intarsia Patterns

This pattern features multiple grain direction arrows, and several colors of wood. I used wengè, yellowheart, and bloodwood. Use soft wood like cedar or poplar for an easier cutting and shaping project. If you don't want to spend a lot of time fitting the inlays in place on the upper wings, just cut the red dotted lines—this opens up the pattern and allows the pieces to slide together tightly. Glue together and sand as one piece.

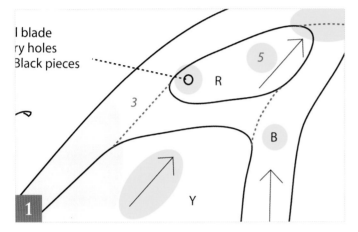

Review symbols: Look your pattern over (page 26), taking note of the different color symbols. The grain direction arrows point in several ways.

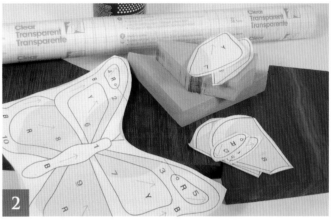

Make copies: Make four copies of the pattern: one for the backer board/work surface, one for the black areas, one for the colored wing sections and one master copy to keep. Cut out all of the black pieces from one pattern. Because the colored sections are not touching, you can cut the red and yellow sections from just one other pattern. Spray the backs of the pattern pieces and stick to the shiny side of the contact paper.

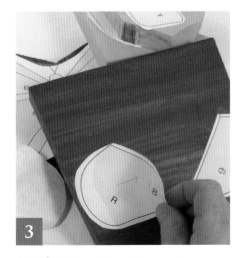

Attach: Cut apart the patterns and group them into same-color piles. Peel the backing off each piece and apply to the correct piece of wood. Line up each pattern with the wood grain according to the arrow direction.

Tips

- One easy way to help find that special area of the board is to cut a window of the section on an extra pattern. You can then move it around the board until you find a section that looks just right. Don't forget to flip over your board and look on the other side as well—grains and color can change from front to back.

- Lay out some of your color wood samples onto your pattern in about the area where they would be. Step back and look at the color combination. Do the colors go together in a harmonious way or do they clash?

- Keep in mind that it is desirable to have flowing grain directions and interesting figured woods in your project. You want the grain patterns to follow the shape of the piece.

- In a good design, the artist includes the plain areas to help make the more complex grain patterns seem more important and interesting to look at.

LESSON 8:
Cutting Multiple-Color Intarsia

Cutting multiple-color intarsia is a slightly more delicate process than cutting a project from just one type of wood. Because you now have pieces from different types fitting together, you have to be particularly careful to cut on the pattern line—otherwise, the pieces will not fit together.

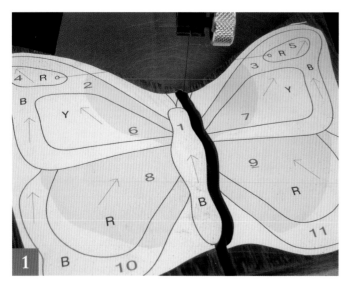

Dark pieces: Cut slowly and stay on your lines, as this will make fitting the color sections easier. Cut the dark sections out. Cutting the butterfly in half along the body makes the pieces easier to handle.

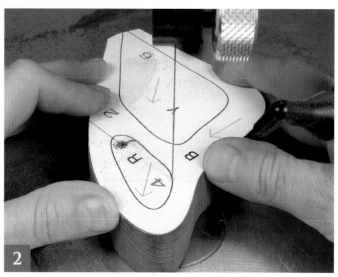

Drill: Drill entry holes in the top wing pieces and cut out the interior spaces.

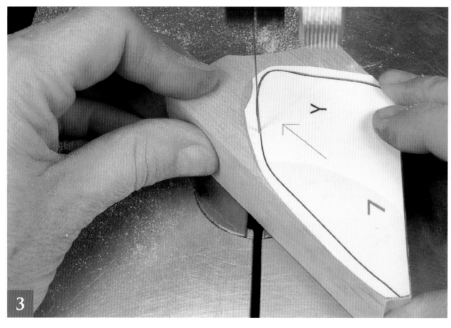

Inlay pieces: Cut each color section out. Be sure not to push the blade; you want a square cut on all your insert pieces. Cut slowly and make your turns carefully. Do not back up and cut if you go off the line—just ease back onto the line.

Tips

- Make sure your blade is square and you'll save a lot of trouble.

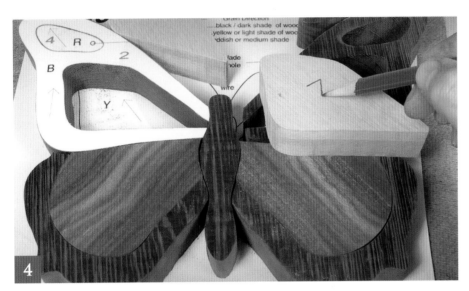

Number: Number each piece on the back with a pencil. At this point, you have all of the pieces cut out.

Cutting for a better fit

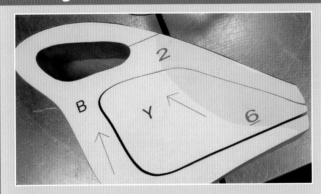

Notice the kerf gap when you remove the inside pieces of the black areas. If you put the cutout waste piece back in place pressed up to one side, there is a two-blade-wide gap on the other side. Be mindful of this when cutting the inlays. Since you had cut on the line for the smaller fitting black waste piece, you will need to cut just outside the line for a closer inlay fit. Be proactive and you won't have to do much refitting later.

LESSON 9:
Creating Simple Color Breaks

The color spots on the wings are treated as color breaks. A color break is not sanded on the edges like other pieces. The edges are flush with surrounding pieces and are sanded as one piece. The technique is used when areas change color but not surface levels, like the spots on a dog.

Fit: Fit each color wing section into the black wing outer frame. If you have a piece that doesn't fit, you will have to make adjustments. First sand all of the sides a little bit on the oscillating sander to make sure all of your edges are square. Lay the colored wing inset on the black wing piece and mark any edges that do not slide in or overhang the edge. Sand the marked edges very slightly on the oscillating sander and re-check your fit. Repeat as many times as needed to fit tightly.

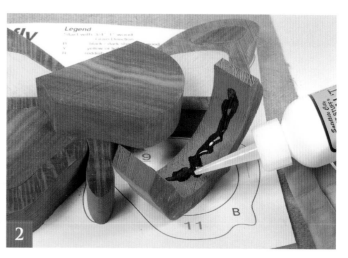

Glue: Use CA glue to tack the colored wing sections in place.

Sand the wings: Once you have all your pieces fitted and glued in place, sand the top flat. Put a slight slope on the bottom wings (shaded parts of 8 and 9) so they appear to be under the top wings. Then put a slope on the top wing edges (shaded parts of 6 and 7) that touch the body so they are lower than the body.

Make a sanding shim

There is another way to make a sanding shim that does not utilize CA glue. This method is time-consuming because you will have to make a separate sanding shim for every large section you want to sand. However, it is always good to know alternative techniques!

Make a shim by tracing the outline of your group of pieces onto a piece of scrap plywood. Cut the plywood out, and using double-stick tape, press your pieces onto the sanding shim. This will support your pieces as one until you are done shaping.

4

Fill gaps: When you have the correct level on your wings, check for any gaps in your inserted sections. You can fix these by mixing a small amount of thick CA glue with dark wood sawdust and scraping it into the gaps with an X-Acto knife. You want to get a thick, slightly runny paste mixture. Then lightly re-sand until the excess glue and sawdust on top is removed. Many repairs will become invisible after the final varnish is applied. Use only for small gaps—larger ones will need another piece cut.

5

Sand: Sand levels into the pieces by rounding the body and the edges of the wings. At this point, the color breaks are in place and you've sanded the levels.

Tips

- If you have a slight gap in your color break areas, you can fix it by using CA glue and sawdust. Catch a bit of the sawdust in a cup while sanding a scrap piece of the darker wood. Mix the sawdust with a few drops of thick CA glue. Let dry about 5 minutes and then sand lightly on the drum sander to remove the extra glue and sawdust. Sand again on the mop and the gap will be almost invisible.

- Be sure to use CA glue in a well-ventilated area. Keep super solvent on hand in case you glue your fingers or take apart an incorrectly glued piece.

LESSON 10:
Fitting Together Multiple-Color Intarsia

Fitting together multiple-color intarsia is as easy as it sounds if you have done the cutting correctly. If not, you will not be able to assemble your intarsia without some extra cutting and sanding. Since multiple-color intarsia involves interlocking pieces cut from different boards, fitting can be tricky. Not to worry—with practice, you'll be able to fit any project together.

1 **Assemble:** Lay out all of the pieces onto your work pattern.

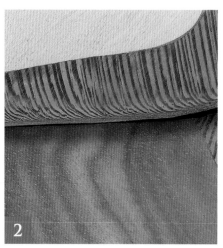

2 **Identify problem fits:** If you have two pieces that do not fit tightly, like the edges of a bottom and top wing, you can recut the line for a tighter fit. The more recutting and trimming you do in one area, the more other areas may misalign, which can lead to even more adjusting. That is why precise cutting is so important.

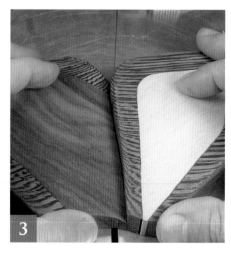

3 **Recut:** Hold the pieces together. Use a #3 skip tooth blade—the thinner blade will bend easily into the gaps. Recut the line between the two pieces. Your blade will cut the tight sections and glide through the gaps. Hold lightly, but press together as you push the pieces into the blade. Practice on scrap pieces before you attempt this skill on your project pieces (see Practice Exercise 5, page 124).

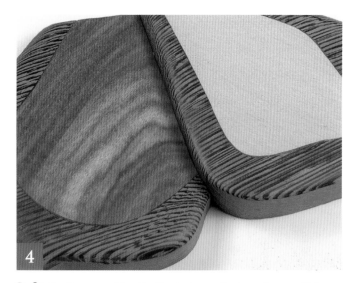

4 **Refit:** Continue recutting the line between the two pieces until there is no longer a gap. Sand all of the pieces on your sanding mop.

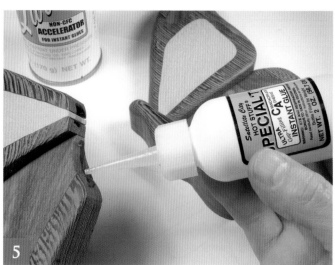

5 **Glue:** Glue the wing pieces together with CA glue and then fit the wings to the body if needed. Glue the rest of your project together as instructed in Lesson 4, page 19. Flat sand the bottom to remove glue and any uneven areas.

Tips

- If a piece doesn't slide into place from either above or below the project, look at the side cuts of that piece and the interlocking piece. Are they perfectly cut at a 90° angle? If you have this problem often, check your blade for squareness.

- If you're having a fit problem, hold one piece on the top of the other. Find the areas that do not fit easily and use a pencil to mark the areas where the pieces touch each other. Sand the places you have marked.

- An oscillating sander is the best tool for evening out edges of slanted pieces. Just touch the edges of the slanted piece, taking care not to sand past the original cut line at the top of your piece.

Finishing the Butterfly

Now your butterfly is ready for finishing. You can paint your backer board or use Masonite and leave it unfinished. Decide what types of finish you want to use. A spray finish is fast and easy to apply.

1 Make the backer board: Place the butterfly onto your backer board pattern and trace the edges. Cut out and sand the edges of the board. Paint the sides and back if you like.

2 Glue: Glue the project to the backer board. Apply dots of CA and wood glue to the project and spray the backer with accelerator. Quickly press the project in place and hold until the CA sets. This will only take a few seconds.

3 Apply spray finish: Use your finish of choice, following the manufacturer's directions. Let dry between coats.

4 Attach hanger: Place a hanger in the middle of the body. Be sure not to drill all the way through to the front and ruin your piece. Screw in the hanger. Drill a small hole in the top of the head and glue in the wire antenna.

This is the finished butterfly.

CHAPTER 3
INTARSIA TECHNIQUES

Now that you know how to handle basic intarsia

projects, you're ready to learn some additional

techniques to advance your intarsia to the next level.

This chapter contains tips and hints from Chapter 4

pattern projects to help you with staining your

project, using shims, and more.

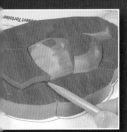
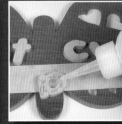

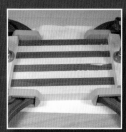

LESSON 11:

Stains

Although I prefer to use natural woods in almost all of my intarsia art, sometimes an intarsia project requires an unavailable or impossible-to-find color. Also, stains and washes allow you to use locally available woods instead of some expensive exotics. Stains are also helpful for beginners, who can cut a project from one piece of wood, stain it, and never worry about fitting multiple colors of wood. Finally, stains can help preserve the colors of some woods—I use dark walnut oil to maintain lovely deep brown shades, and white gel stain to keep white woods from turning brown with age.

Creating stain samples

Always test any stain or color wash before you put it on your completed project. Sometimes it may take several attempts to get the right color and you don't want to ruin your project pieces. Cut several strips of the wood used in the project, and sand them as you would your project pieces.

Each time you use a wash or new stain, make a sample wood strip and mark on the back what you used to get that color. After a while you will have an extensive catalog of stained or color-washed wood samples. It will save time and be a great help when deciding what colors or woods will be the perfect choice for a particular project.

Food dye

To use food dye on your project, add a few drops to a small amount of water. The more drops of dye, the more intense the color will be. Don't make the color too deep, or your wood grain will disappear completely. The water may raise the grain of some soft woods, such as poplar. If this occurs, lightly sand the wood with very fine sandpaper after it is dry.

Acrylic paint

Acrylic paint is best applied as a wash—straight paint will obscure wood grain. Start with a small amount of water and add a bit of acrylic paint. Mix well. Test several concentrations of the wash until you are happy with the results.

Oil stain

Oil stain looks best when thinned with mineral spirits. Add a small amount of pigment to some mineral spirits. Stir, paint the mixture on the test strip, and wipe it off immediately. It is a good idea to put a second or third coat on one end of the test strip to see how the stain looks when applied heavier.

Application of stain

Divide your piece into color groups and paint on the stains using a small brush. Wipe it off and let dry overnight. If the grain raises and the surface feels rough, you will have to lightly sand it down with fine sandpaper or steel wool. Be careful not to remove the stain by sanding, unless that is the effect you are looking for.

I tested blue food dye, acrylic paint, and oil stain for the USA keyholder (pattern on page 56).

I used water-based color stains to add color to the Train Photo Frame (pattern on page 70).

LESSON 12:

Using Shims to Add a 3-D Effect

A shim is a thin piece of wood, usually plywood, that is placed under one or more pieces of your intarsia in order to raise those pieces above the surrounding pieces. Shims are the same shape as the piece or pieces they will raise, but slightly smaller. In this lesson, you will learn how and when to add a riser or shim to your project to give it more depth. The patterns in this book have shim suggestions, marked with red dotted lines. However, you should always look over your project and see if there are any other areas that would look good raised. Areas that are highest or appear closest to you will be the best ones to add a riser to. The areas must be located in the middle of other pieces and not at the edge of the project—otherwise, your riser will show.

The following steps, performed while creating the Tortoise (pattern on page 68), show the use of a large shim to raise an entire section of pieces and a small shim for one piece.

1

Cut: Cut out your shims using ⅜" (10mm) plywood or flat scrap wood after you have cut out the rest of the intarsia pieces. Cut on the dotted red line, keeping inside the area. Mark your shim with "UP" so you don't glue the wrong side later. Since you cut the shim to fit under certain pieces, if you flip it over accidentally it will not fit correctly.

2

Attach secondary shims: If the project has any shimmed pieces on top of a larger shim, attach them now with CA glue. For example, the middle shell piece in the Tortoise project has a shim. The shell has three levels: the middle piece is highest, then the rest of the shimmed shell, and the lowest pieces are around the large shim.

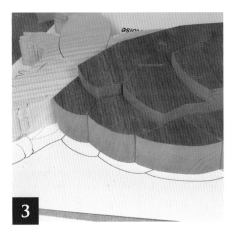

3

Test fit: Lay your pieces on your workboard with the shims in place.

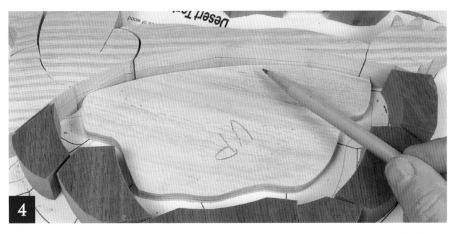

4

Sand: Remove the pieces that will be on the shim. Use the shim as a gauge to mark the level on all the pieces surrounding the raised area. This is the line you must not go below when sanding, or else you will expose the shim. Sand the pieces of your project.

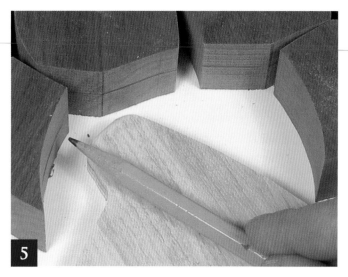

5

Mark: If you have any secondary shims, be sure to mark the shim level on the pieces around it as well. You never want to sand surrounding pieces lower than the shim, or you will be able to see the shim.

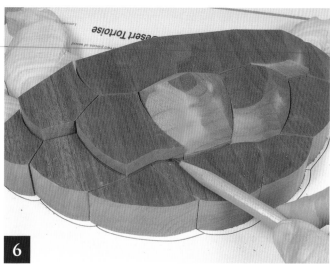

6

Create flow: Lay the pieces back in place on the workboard and mark lines at the edges of the raised pieces. Sand down to these lines to make your pieces flow from the higher level to the lower un-shimmed pieces. Do not remove any wood from the lower pieces.

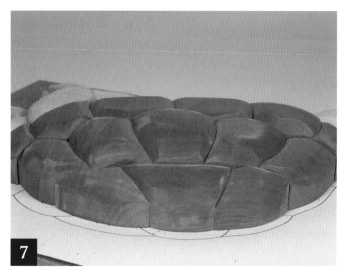

7

Sand each piece: Sand all the pieces on and around the shims. If two pieces don't meet, use your pencil to mark the higher piece and sand down slightly to that level. Mark, sand, fit, and repeat.

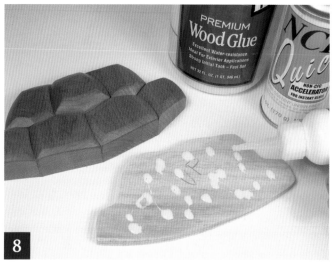

8

Glue the large shim: Glue the pieces that will be shimmed together with CA glue. Use wood glue, CA glue, and accelerator to glue them to the riser. Make sure the edges of the riser are not exposed at the sides. Complete project as desired.

Tips

- Make sure your shim is clean, flat, and sanded smooth for a good surface to glue onto.

- Experiment with several thicknesses of shim wood to get the level of riser that looks best.

LESSON 13:
Using Overlays

Adding overlay pieces to your intarsia will really make it pop. Overlays are simply pieces of the intarsia that are glued on top of other parts to create height, especially in areas where a shim cannot be used. For instance, the Frog (pattern on page 84) and Raccoon projects (pattern on page 104) have overlays that create a 3-D effect to the entire piece. An easy way to utilize overlays is to add lettering to your projects.

1

Cut: Cut out the project pieces. Sand the surface and edges. Make sure your surfaces are clean, dry, and flat—so the overlays will lay flat. Cut out the overlays.

2

Sand and glue: Sand and lay out the pieces. Put a line or small dots of CA glue on the bottom of your overlays. Don't use too much glue or it will ooze out and look messy.

Tips

■ Cut each letter out of ⅛" or ¼" (3mm or 6mm) stock. Drill all holes first and cut out the inside of letters before you cut the outline; you will have more wood to hold on to.

■ Use needle-nose pliers or forceps to hold the small letters for sanding and placement.

■ Take a piece of masking tape and use it to make a straight line at the bottom of your letters. This will be your guide to keep the letters straight. Glue the middle letter first so the name is centered.

Materials

■ 8" x 5" x ⅜" (203mm x 127mm x 10mm) red wood (redwood)

■ 3" x 8" x ⅛" or ¼" (76mm x 203mm x 3mm or 6mm) light wood (poplar)

Letters are overlays

Use the letters on page 117 or make your own.

100%

LEGEND

→   Grain direction
R   Red wood
L   Light or white wood (stain any color you wish)
- - - - -   Line to align letters

LESSON 14:
Making a Lamination

A lamination is created by gluing together pieces of wood to make a design—such as the red and white stripes in the USA keyholder pattern (page 56)—before final cutting is done.

I used this technique on my turkey intarsia (photo at right). You can also get some interesting effects for landscapes by laminating several colors of wood. For example, the stripes in the USA pattern could be cut out one at a time and sanded individually, but this would take a lot of time and effort. For an interesting and easy effect, you can glue your stripes first before you cut out the letters. See how to do this below.

Lamination worked well for the black and white feathers on my turkey intarsia.

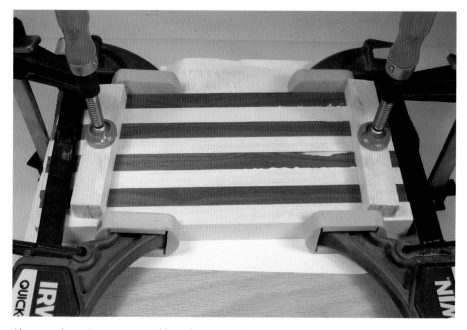

Alternate the strips on your workboard. Put wood glue between each board and clamp tightly together. Put a piece of paper underneath the wood strips and set on a flat board. Clamp down from the top as well to ensure a flat finished slab of striped wood. Let dry overnight.

LESSON 15:
Woodburning Texture

A woodburner is a wonderful tool that can be used to add detail and interest to your projects. An adjustable temperature is a great feature that allows you more control for deep burning or just light accents. Woodburning tips come in many styles, each one designed for a particular function. Some are for shading, adding feathers/fur, writing, or fine sharp lines. Each woodburning tip will burn differently at the same setting. Each type of wood will burn differently, so always practice on a scrap piece of your project wood before you start woodburning your project. You can use a lower setting to avoid the burnt edges. You can get a deeper line with a higher setting and touch the pieces on a sanding mop to soften the lines and remove the excessively burnt areas. On hard dark wood, such as black walnut, excessively burnt areas will blend into the background when varnished. For this woodburning lesson, we will use the Tortoise project (pattern on page 68).

Use a sharp fine point for the stitching on the Cowboy Boot Clock project (pattern on page 90).

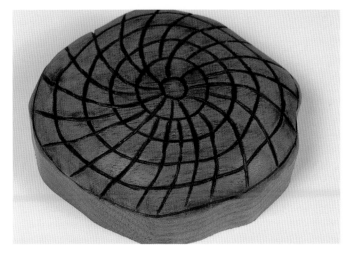

The center of the Sunflower project (pattern on page 88) can be woodburned for a neat effect.

Using a woodburner is a great way to create texture on hair.

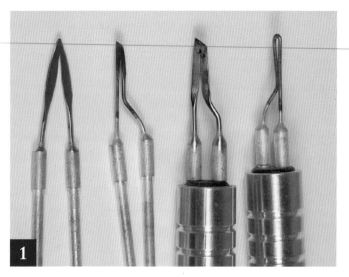

Experiment: Test different temperature settings on a scrap piece of wood from your project. Try different tips to find the one that works best for the project and wood you are using. The small or large knife tip is a good universal tip for many projects.

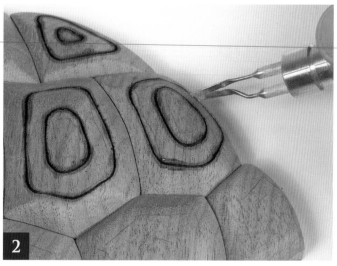

Mark and burn: Mark the lines lightly in pencil on your wood before you start to burn. Burn any desired details.

Shade: Use a flat tip for filling in and shading any small areas, such as the toenails on the Tortoise project. This will save you from cutting out small areas from a darker wood and fitting them in place. Use the sanding mop to remove the excess burned edges of the lines.

LESSON 16:
Carving Texture

Power and hand carving are both options to add texture to your intarsia. As with any technique, take the time to experiment on scrap wood to see which bits and knives work best for the details you are carving and the wood you are using. Practice the same carving lines you will be putting on your pieces, using the same type of wood. Putting deep cuts in your pieces will allow shadows to form, which gives the illusion of more depth than is actually there.

The tail on the Raccoon project (pattern on page 104) is the perfect palette for some extreme carving texture. Follow along as I shape the tail sections. I will be using a power die grinder with a fine bit. Power carving bits, also known as burrs, come in many shapes designed for different shaping effects—including cone, taper, cylinder, and ball nose. Burrs come in coarse, medium, and fine styles, and are available in many shank diameters from 1/16" to 1/2" (2mm to 13mm). Some leave a smooth finish on the wood while others are for fast removal of wood, cutting, and sanding. Buy several styles and sizes. After using the burrs, you can use a 120- or 220-grit sanding sleeve or a sanding stone in a fine grit to smooth the rough areas. The sanding sleeves fit over 1/4" or 1/2" (6mm or 13mm) mandrels. Mini sanding mops are a good addition to your burr collection; they can make woodworking more enjoyable by eliminating hand sanding.

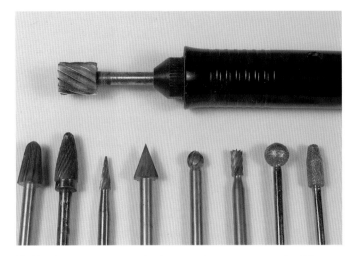

Carbine burrs are very popular because they remove wood quicker than other burrs and leave a smooth surface.

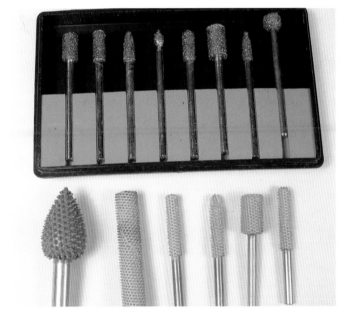

SaburrTooth carbide-coated burrs work very nice for quick wood removal.

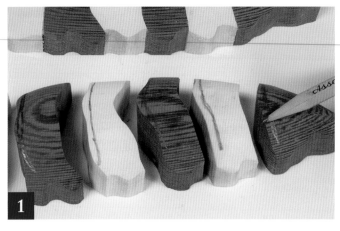

Tack: Use CA glue to tack the pieces together and round the entire section on the sander. Break the pieces apart and sand each section so its level fits under the next section.

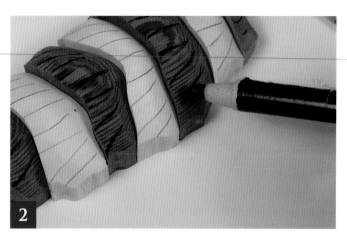

Mark: Mark all of your pieces with a pencil line in the direction you want to carve.

Power carve: Use the rotary tool of your choice for the deep carving. I used a SaburrTooth fine ⅛" (3mm) taper. Carefully hold your piece in place on a hard surface and carve any deep valleys from the top to bottom.

Sand: Sand the sections on the sanding mop to help remove rough edges. Use a sanding sleeve or a sanding stone with a sharp edge to clean out any valleys. Here, I am using the very top edge of a cylinder-shaped stone to add fine lines along each cut.

Hand carve: Use a carving knife to add sharp cuts. Touch up on the sanding mop one final time. Now the pieces are ready to be glued up and attached to the rest of the project.

LESSON 17:
Using CA Glue

CA glue (cyanoacrylate adhesive) is one of the best time-saving products you can use. Trade names include Hot Stuff, Zap, Crazy Glue, and others. They come in a variety of formulas for different applications and setting times. Thin, medium, and thick glues have setting times from three to thirty seconds. You can also purchase odorless CA glue, called UFO glue; it is more expensive than regular CA glue, but may be worth the extra money.

CA bonds can be so strong that the wood will actually tear apart before your glued seam will break. I use CA glue in several ways: for sanding, gap filling, gluing projects together, and for gluing backer boards to my projects. CA accelerator speeds up setting time, making short work of gluing. You must also keep CA solvent on hand. It is great for un-bonding misaligned pieces and removing glue from your fingers.

> **Caution!** CA glue can cause allergic skin reactions and is an eye and respiratory irritant. Use adequate ventilation!

CA glue for sanding

This is my favorite method for sanding several pieces together—very fast and easy. I use it 95% of the time. Put two or three small dots of thick CA glue near the bottom of one piece. Spray the opposite side with accelerator and fit back together. You can use spray accelerator if you want to hurry up the process. Just make sure you get your pieces in the right place and flat quickly. Without the accelerator, setting time is about one minute; with the spray, you will have about five to ten seconds to get your pieces positioned correctly. As you become more comfortable using this method, you will use the accelerator more often. Press your pieces together tightly on top of a very flat surface covered with paper. Because you are gluing at the bottom of your pieces, sometimes your glue will leak down and adhere to the work surface. Paper will sand off the back of your pieces easily. Wax paper is a good choice.

Glue: Use CA to glue together the pieces you want to sand.

Sand and Separate: Sand the group of pieces as desired. When done sanding, simply rap the pieces on a hard surface to break them apart.

As you are holding the two pieces together, twist them as the glue sets. Twisting will prevent it from sticking to the paper. It will only take about five to ten seconds to set up completely so you have to work quickly. Add on any other pieces one at a time if you are tacking a group of pieces. Now your pieces are glued together and you can sand the entire contour as you wish. If your piece comes apart while you are sanding, re-glue in a different area. You may have not used enough glue or glued at a point where the two pieces were not tightly joined. To take the pieces apart, simply rap the pieces on a hard surface and they will break apart. Practice on some scrap wood before you try it out on your projects pieces. If the pieces don't come apart easily, you used too much glue. Use CA solvent in the seams first to loosen the glue. If it still won't come apart, you will have to recut the seam on the pieces. Clean off any CA glue in your seams by X-Acto knife. Small, fragile, or delicate pieces should not be used with this method. Once you master using the CA glue tacking method, you may never make another sanding shim.

4

CHAPTER 4

PROJECTS

This chapter contains intarsia projects to spur your

creativity. Try creating the Sunflower (page 88), the

Raccoon (page 104), or the Beagle Puppy (page 66).

LEVEL 1

LEVEL 1 STEP-BY-STEP PROJECT:
Iris

This project is stack-cut from a light and dark piece of ⅝"- (16mm-) thick wood. Stack-cutting means that two or more pieces of wood are stacked on top of each other and held together. Stack-cutting allows you to make two projects in the time it takes to cut out one. Since you cut both colors at the same time, you can make a project with two colors of wood and the pieces will fit, even if you wandered off the line a bit. I used black walnut and bird's-eye maple, but I recommend soft woods, such as cedar or poplar, for beginners.

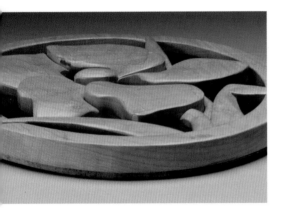

Materials

- 8" x 10" x ⅝" or ¾" (203mm x 254mm x 16mm or 19mm) light or medium wood (bird's-eye maple or poplar)
- 8" x 10" x ⅝" or ¾" (203mm x 254mm x 16mm or 19mm) dark contrasting wood (black walnut or cedar)
- ¼" (6mm) backer board, 2
- 8" x 8" x ¹⁄₁₆" (203mm x 203mm x 2mm) plywood, 2

Tips

- You can have the grain of the two pieces of wood in the same direction, or turn one piece sideways for a different look.

- Make a practice cut on two pieces of your wood and if it seems too hard to cut, use thinner wood. Using thinner wood will be easier to cut, but you will not be able to get a lot of depth in your shaping.

- Remember to let the blade cut the wood at its own speed—don't push the wood too hard into the blade or you will bend the blade and your bottom pieces will not properly fit into your top pieces.

- If you stray off the line, don't back cut, but ease back onto the line.

- If you want to cut only one iris project, stack cut one piece of ⅝" or ¾" (16mm or 19mm) wood and one piece of contrasting ¼"- (6mm-) thick wood for the background. It will save time, as you won't have to sand the background pieces down to the correct height.

LEVEL 1

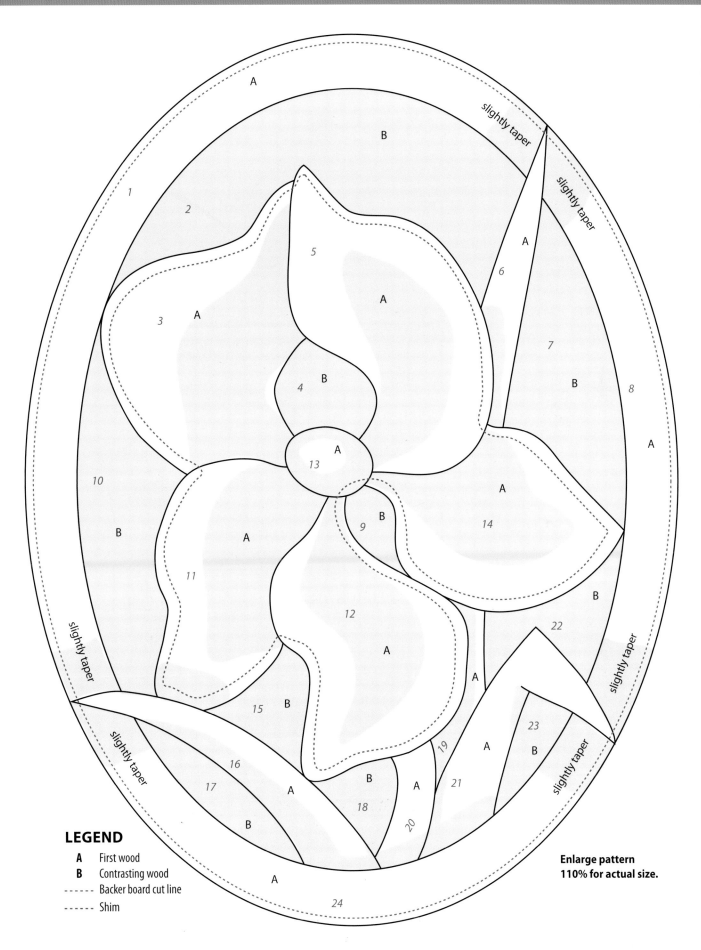

A

B

slightly taper

slightly taper

1

2

5

A

6

A

3   A

7

A

4   B

B   8

A

13   A

10

B   A   14

B

9   B

11

B   22

12

A

A

slightly taper

slightly taper

A

15   B

23

19   A   B

slightly taper

16

17   A   21

B

18   A

A   20

slightly taper

LEGEND

A   First wood
B   Contrasting wood
- - - -   Backer board cut line
- - - -   Shim

A

**Enlarge pattern
110% for actual size.**

24

LEVEL 1

LEVEL 1 STEP-BY-STEP PROJECT: IRIS

1

Copy pattern: Make two copies of the iris pattern. Use one for the backer board and one for the stacked wood. Spray the backside of the pattern piece with spray adhesive. Stick the patterns onto the shiny side of the contact paper.

2

Prepare backer boards: Select two pieces of Masonite for your backer boards. Using double-stick carpet tape (Duck Brand Light Traffic works well), tape the two boards together with the rough sides up. Tape the edges together with regular tape if needed. Peel and stick one pattern onto the boards.

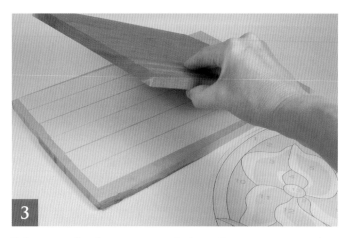

3

Select wood: Select two pieces of ⅝" or ¾" (16mm or 19mm) soft wood of contrasting colors. Look for interesting grain and color. Make sure they are the same thickness and flat. Plane them if needed. Attach the two pieces with double-stick carpet tape.

4

Attach pattern: Make sure your wood is clean and free of dust. Tape the edges together with regular tape if your two pieces are not tight. Peel the backing off and stick the other iris pattern onto your boards.

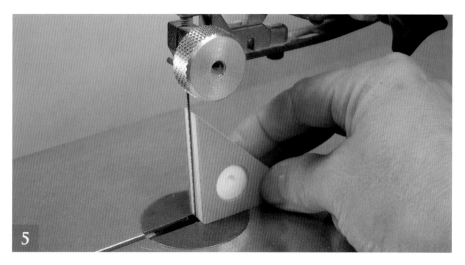

5

Square your blade: Check your blade for squareness to the table. I use a regular skip tooth #5 blade because it cuts thick wood well. Sand the burr on the bottom after each cut and your wood will remain flat as you cut.

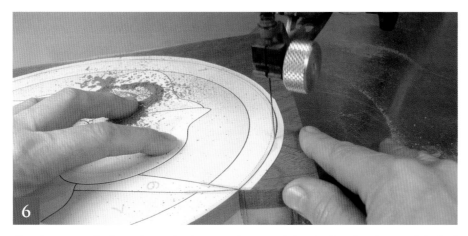

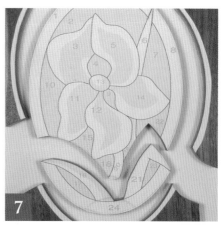

Cut the outer circle: Make two back-up cuts (cut in and then back out) at the top of the leaf (6) to free up pieces 1 and 8 when you cut the inner circle. Check the tape. If your pieces slip, you will not get a tight fit.

Cut above 16 and 21: Cut across the bottom at the top of the leaves (16, 21).

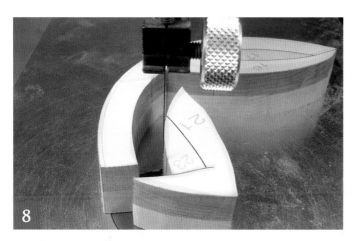

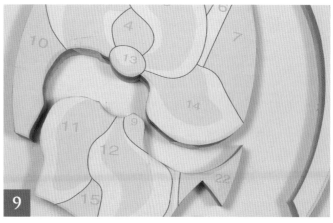

Cut the inner circle: Cut the inner frame circle. Make a back-up cut on the leaf (21) and cut the inner frame piece at the bottom (24). Cut slowly when you reach the back-up line—you don't want to cut into the side of the leaf.

Cut the middle: Cut across the middle of your flower, starting at the left bottom of piece 11. Continue across the bottom of the middle piece (13) and the bottom of the right petal (14).

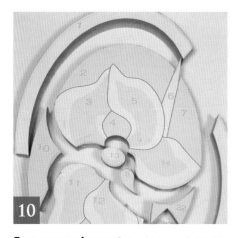

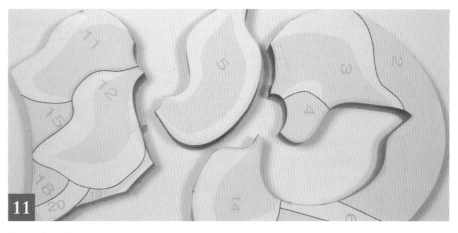

Free some pieces: Cut out pieces 9, 10, 13, 17, 22, and 23.

Free piece 5: Cut piece 5 out of the larger section, making the sharp turn at the top of the petal. Cut the line between 11 and 12.

LEVEL 1 STEP-BY-STEP PROJECT: **IRIS**

Number: Lay out your cut pieces on top of the backer board pattern. Take the stack-cut pieces apart and use a pencil to number each one on the bottom.

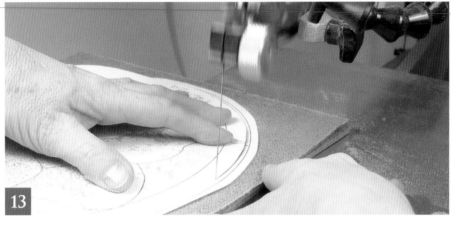

Cut the backer boards: Cut on the blue dotted line. I recommend a reverse tooth blade, which leaves a clean bottom and works well for thin boards. Remove the pattern and tape. Sand and stain the edges if needed. Mark the rough side as the top.

Lay out: Lay out your two irises on the backer boards. Exchange the background pieces (2, 4, 7, 9, 10, 15, 17–18, 22, 23). Select one of the projects to continue with. You can complete the second one after finishing the first.

Mark sanding areas: Mark the areas to sand with a pencil using the gray areas on the pattern as a sanding guide. These will become the lower areas of the iris.

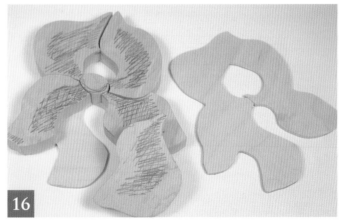

Cut risers: Stack-cut two pieces of 1⁄16" plywood to serve as risers behind the flower (3, 5, 11–14). Sand the edges and sides clean. Check the height of the riser next to a background piece and put the risers in place.

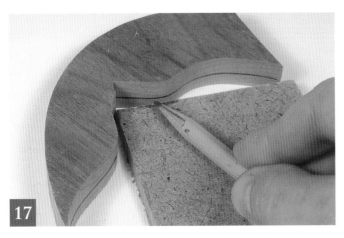

17

Mark the background: Mark all the sides of the background pieces using a ³⁄₁₆"- (5mm-) thick piece of scrap wood. The background is the lowest part of the design.

18

Sand the background: Sand all of the background pieces by taking down the wood to the lines on all four sides.

Sanding

I like using a pneumatic drum sander, but you can use whatever sanding method you have available. A Dremel or die grinder with a sanding band or burr, an osculating sander, or a belt sander would all work. Push the piece into the drum with light pressure to remove a small amount of material and harder to remove more. I use rough 100 grit on my 8" (203mm) sanding drum first, then I go to my 2" (51mm) sanding drum with 180 grit for a nice finish-sanded surface. When sanding, wear rubber finger tip protectors. Use tweezers or needle-nose pliers to hold the small pieces.

If you find the small pieces are difficult to hold, try using a sanding shim. Take double-sided carpet tape and adhere the small piece to a piece of scrap wood. This will give you something larger to hold on to while sanding. Make sure there is no dust on the

wood when you put the tape on. You can also use a few drops of CA glue and accelerator to tack the piece to a larger piece of wood. Don't use too much glue, or you will crack the wood when you take it apart. If the pieces do not pull apart easily, use some CA solvent in the seam and it will pull apart.

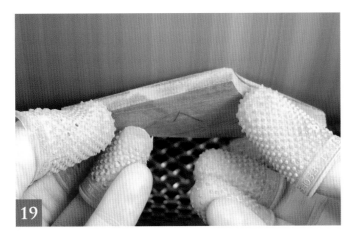

19

Finish sanding the background: Take down the center to make a nice flat surface. Place the pieces back onto the pattern. Lay out all of your pieces on the backer board and check the levels of your background pieces. Make any adjustments needed.

20

Begin to shape: Mark the edge of the left petal (11). Sand to this line, but not below. Replace pieces often while sanding. Remove the bottom outer frame (24). Mark the levels of the leaves and sand. Slightly round the edges of the iris center (13).

LEVEL 1 STEP-BY-STEP PROJECT: **IRIS**

21

Sand the leaves: Finish sanding the leaves and stems, being careful not to sand below the riser. Mark and replace the pieces to check levels often.

22

Sand the petals: Create a nice flowing slope to the petals. The 2" (51mm) sanding drum makes a nice concave slope to the inside of the petals. Put the pieces together. Have you achieved the necessary depth?

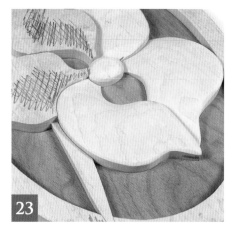

23

Continue sanding: Mark and sand pieces 5 and 6. Watch your shim while sanding the leaf. Remember, take off a little at a time: once it is off you can't put it back.

24

Sand the frame: Lay out your pieces. Sand the frame near the overlapping leaves. Slightly round the edges. You will need the smaller 2" sanding drum (51mm) or a Dremel for the inside curve. Are you satisfied with the depths and overall look of your piece?

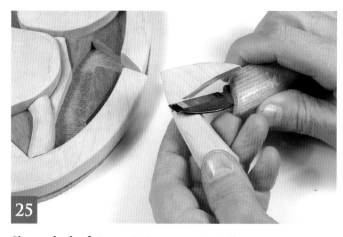

25

Shape the leaf: Use a grinder or a carving knife to cut the area under the bend of leaf 21.

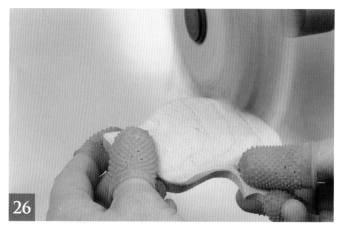

26

Sand with the mop: The sanding mop saves much time and effort. I use a 150 grit first and then a 220 grit. It only takes a few moments to get a beautiful finish. If you used soft wood, make sure your RPM is low so you don't burn the wood.

27

Glue the frame: Place the pieces on the board. Remove the bottom frame (24) and apply dots of wood and CA glue. Spray the backer board with accelerator and carefully replace 24. Press down for a few seconds. Attach the rest of the frame (1, 8).

28

Glue the iris shim: Using dots of wood and CA glues, attach the petals and center (3, 5, 11–14), one at a time, to the shim. Leave the other pieces in place but unglued. Be careful not to use too much glue—it will squeeze out.

29

Glue the iris: Lift out the shimmed iris. Use dots of wood glue and CA to glue it to the backer board. Do not glue the internal background (4, 9). Move the iris into the center if there are gaps—this way, they will be spread out.

30

Glue the rest: Glue the background pieces (2, 4, 7, 9, 10, 15, 17–18, 22, 23) and bottom leaves (16, 20, 21) in place one at a time. Watch that you do not use so much glue that it leaks through the cracks.

Finish: Trim any overhanging backer boards and straighten up the outside edges if needed. Spray several coats of varnish on your projects. Attach the hanger on back and admire your intarsia piece.

31

USA Keyholder

Materials

- 11" x 6" x 1" (279mm x 152mm x 25mm) red wood (bloodwood)
- 18" x 6" x 1" (457mm x 152mm x 25mm) white wood (poplar)
- Blue stain of choice

Tips

- You can use red wood or cedar for the red strips.

- Cut the red and white strips on your table saw. Each strip should be 11" long x 1" wide x ⅝" high (279mm x 25mm x 16mm).

- Use a rotary carving tool to sand the inside curves and edges of the star.

- Blue wood the color of the flag is impossible to find, so stains or washes are the only way to go with this project. I choose blue oil paint wash because I liked the way the wood grain showed through but the color was still a strong blue.

- If you choose to use blue oil paint, brush it on and wipe it off right away.

- See further instruction in Lesson 14, page 40.

LEVEL 1

LEGEND
→   Grain direction
B   Blue stain or wash
R   Red shade
W   White shade

⅝" x 1" x 11
4 red & 4 white

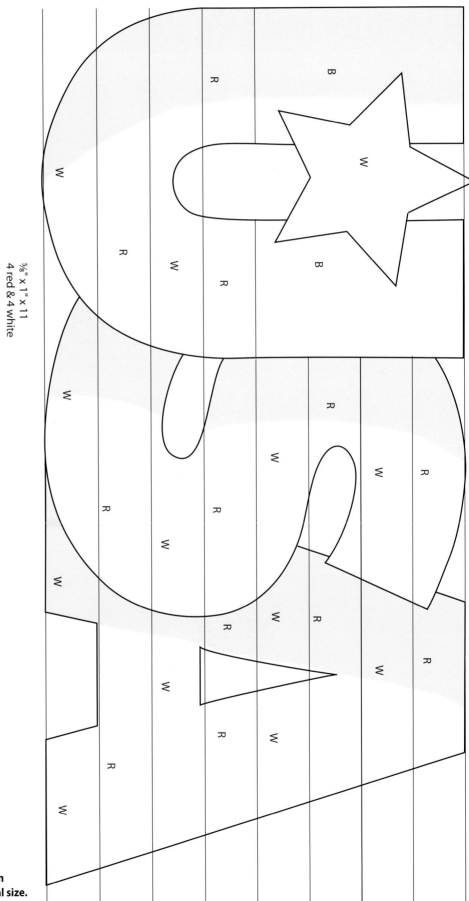

**Enlarge pattern
110% for actual size.**

Baseball Mitt Picture Frame

Materials

- 9' (229mm) round leather lacing
- 11" x 12" x ¾" (279mm x 305mm x 19mm) medium wood (cherry)
- 4" x 4" x 1" (102mm x 102 x 25mm) white wood (poplar)
- ⅛" (3mm) drill bit
- Awl for cleaning holes

Tips

- If you don't have a wide enough board to cut the mitt out in one piece, separate the pattern into two pieces: 1, 2, 7 and 3, 4, 5, 6.

- Sand a slight concave slope into piece 7 from the top of the ball towards section 1.

- On piece 6, sand a sharp angle toward the ball.

- Stack cut the backer board pieces using double-sided carpet tape in between. Cut the red dotted line around the entire outside of the mitt. Take the pieces apart and cut the photo insert area on the top piece only. Sand the edges if needed and glue the two pieces back together.

- Mark all of the holes by eye or lay a pattern over the pieces and mark with a nail imprint. Drill each hole with a ⅛" (3mm)

drill bit all the way through. Sand the bottom of each piece to remove the drill hole burr.

- Use a woodburner to make the stitching marks on the ball.

- You can cut all of the lacing into smaller pieces, insert, and glue or actually lace through the mitt like I did.

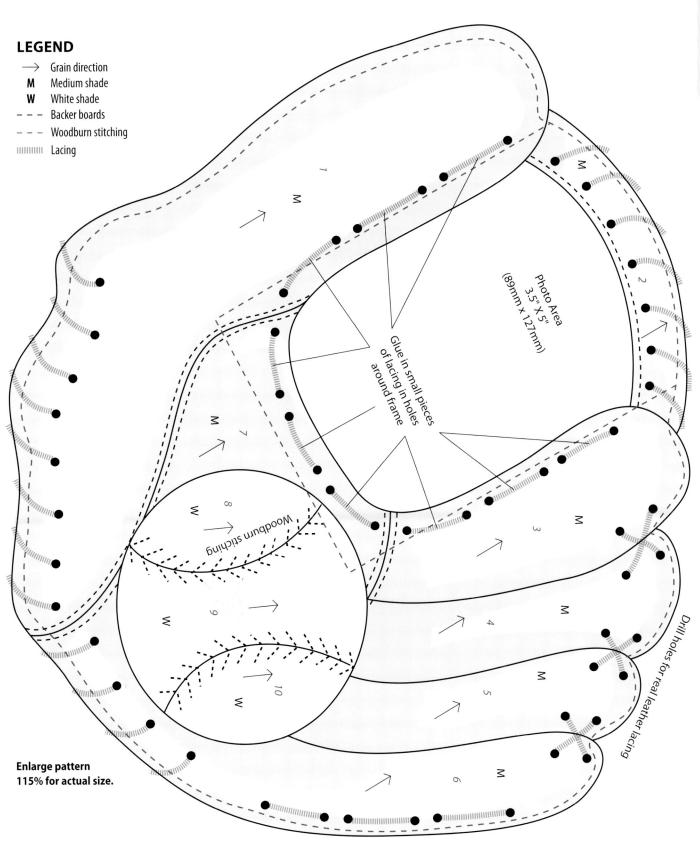

LEGEND

→ Grain direction
M Medium shade
W White shade
– – – Backer boards
– – – Woodburn stitching
|||||||||| Lacing

Photo Area
3.5" x 5"
(89mm x 127mm)

Glue in small pieces
of lacing in holes
around frame

Woodburn stitching

Drill holes for real leather lacing

**Enlarge pattern
115% for actual size.**

LEVEL 1

Angel

Materials

- 6" x 6" x 1" (152mm x 152mm x 25mm) medium wood (cherry)
- 10" x 8" x 1" (254mm x 203mm x 25mm) white wood (poplar)
- 5" x 1" x 1" (127mm x 25mm x 25mm) yellow wood (yellowheart)

Tips

- A rotary carving tool works great to add the details to the face, gown, hands, and wings. You can also use a new X-Acto blade or a carving knife. Wearing a carving glove to protect your fingers from cuts is a good idea.

- Woodburn the black section of the eye.

- By using white oak gel stain, you can get a nice soft contrast between the gown and the face and hand sections.

- I added a coat of iridescent medium pearl acrylic paint to the gown and wing after staining for a beautiful result. If you like, you can add glitter to the wing piece for a sparkly effect. Have fun with this little angel!

LEGEND

→ Grain direction
B Black or dark shade
M Medium shade
L Light shade
W White shade
Y Yellow shade

Ornament size

100%

LEVEL 1

Mice and Cheese

Materials

- 7" x 6" x 1" (178mm x 152mm x 25mm) medium wood (beech)
- 5" x 3" x ½" (127mm x 76mm x 13mm) light wood, tails (sycamore)
- 2" x 1" x 1" (51mm x 25mm x 25mm) light wood, ears (sycamore)
- 9" x 7" x ¾" (229mm x 178mm x 19mm) yellow wood (yellowheart)
- 2" x 1" x ¼" (51mm x 25mm x 6mm) black wood, eyes (ebony)

Tips

To use a drum sander on thin pieces, hold them downward with a shim supporting the back.

- Drill and cut out the eye areas and cut the eyes from ebony or woodburn them.

- If your right mouse doesn't fit in easily, you can cut the extra hole (red dotted line) near the head.

- Use a hard wood, like maple, for the delicate tails.

- Test for a flat fit by placing the tail in place. Make any adjustments needed so your tail will glue flat on both the foot and the cheese.

- Use an oscillating sander to shape the tails. Make sure you don't push too hard as the wood becomes thinner.

- Use wood hardener to make your delicate pieces harder and less prone to breakage.

- You can use wire or leather for the tails.

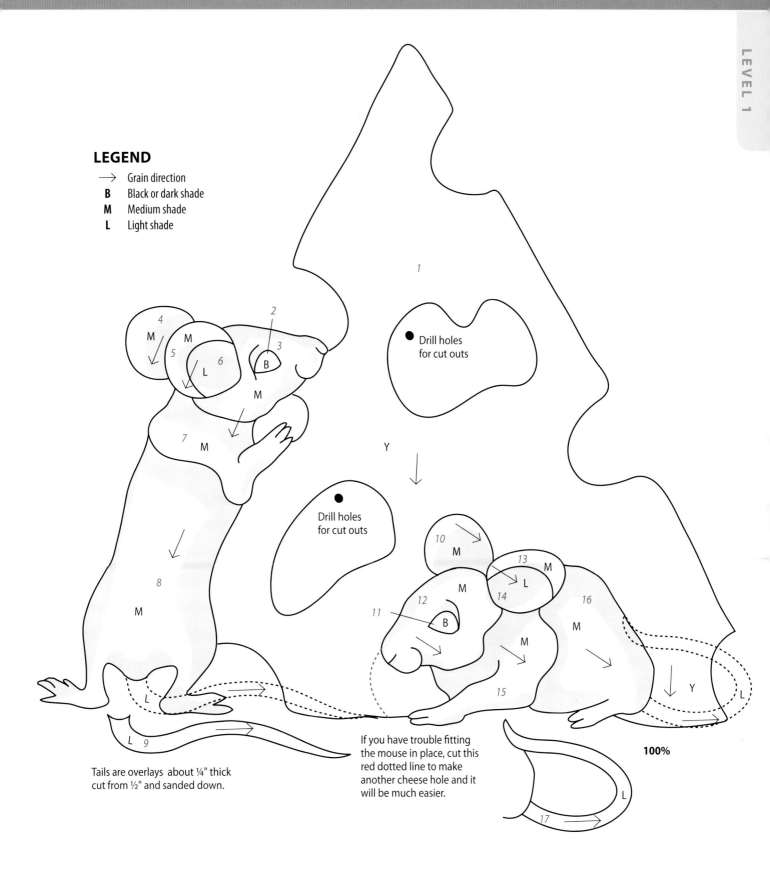

LEGEND
→ Grain direction
B Black or dark shade
M Medium shade
L Light shade

1

● Drill holes
for cut outs

2

4

M

M

5

L *6*

B *3*

M

7 M

Y

● Drill holes
for cut outs

10

M

13 M

8

M

12 M

L

11 B

14

16

M

M

15

L

Y

L *9*

Tails are overlays about ¼" thick
cut from ½" and sanded down.

If you have trouble fitting
the mouse in place, cut this
red dotted line to make
another cheese hole and it
will be much easier.

100%

L

17

Cat

Materials

- 7" x 6" x 1" (178mm x 152mm x 25mm) black or dark wood (black walnut)

- 2" x 2" x 1" (51mm x 51mm x 25mm) medium-dark wood (light black walnut or beech)

- 2" x 1" x 1" (51mm x 25mm x 25mm) medium wood, nose (beech)

- 5" x 3" x ½" (127mm x 76mm x 13mm) white wood (poplar)

- 1" x 1" x 1" (25mm x 25mm x 25mm) yellow wood, eye (yellowheart)

Tips

- Pay special attention to the red lines where the color breaks are. You will need to stay on the lines as carefully as you can. Good cutting here will make fitting your color breaks much easier.

- Use a rotary tool to slightly round the inside edges of the tail. Taper the base of the tail down to go behind the rear haunch of the cat.

- Make the area next to the tail lower to help the tail seem higher.

- Sand pieces 16 and 13 so they are lower than the surrounding pieces.

- Shape the small eyebrow piece. Use pliers or forceps to hold the small piece. You can use the rotary tool or oscillating sander if you have trouble using the larger drum sander.

LEVEL 1

LEGEND

→   Grain direction
B   Black shade
D   Dark shade
MD   Medium-dark shade
M   Medium shade
W   White shade
Y   Yellow shade
–¼   ¼" (6mm) sand down or thinner wood
——   Color breaks

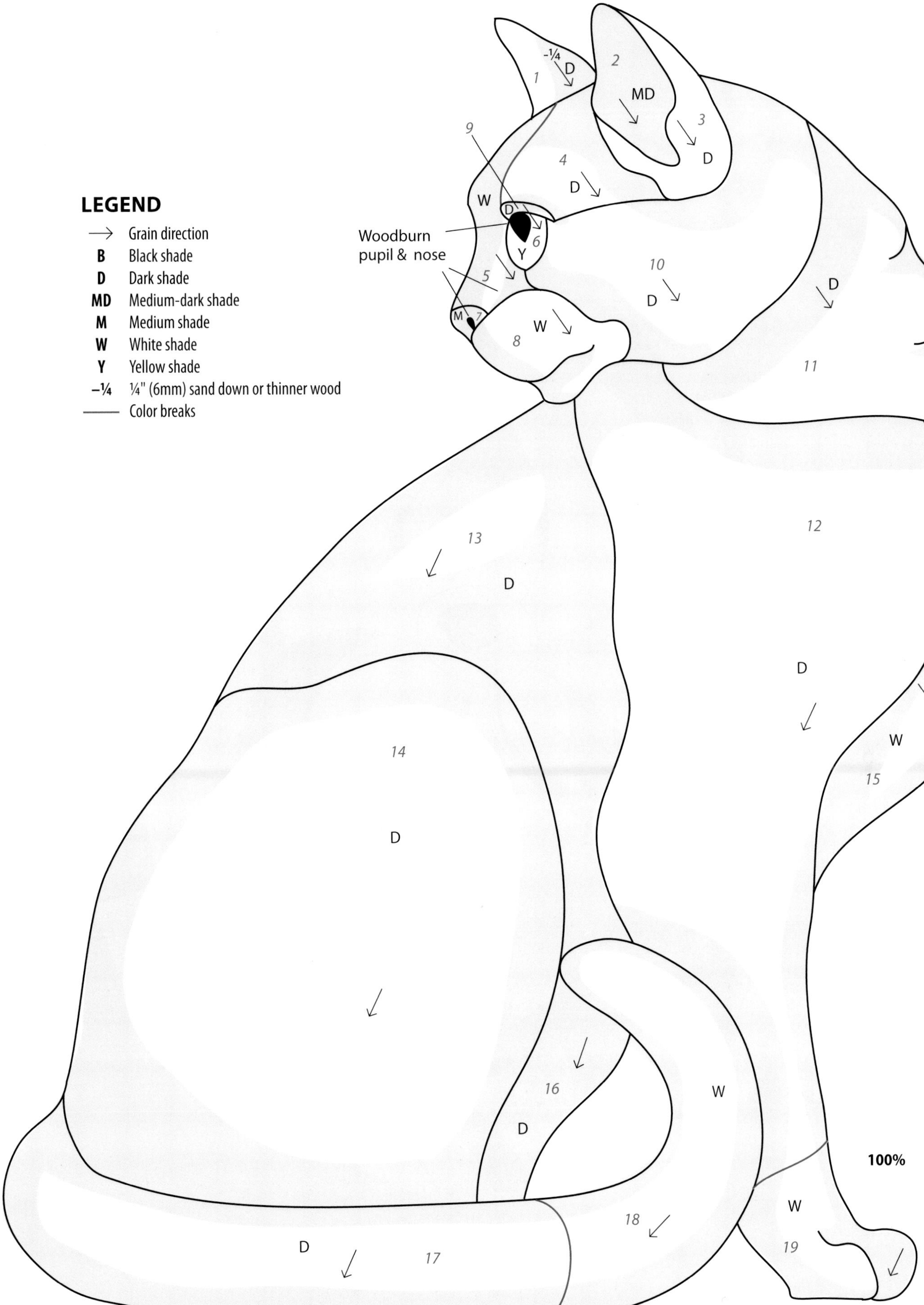

Woodburn
pupil & nose

LEVEL 1

Beagle Puppy

Tips

- Pay special attention to the red lines on the pattern—the color breaks. Precise cutting here will make fitting pieces together a snap.

- Taper the top part of the front leg to go down under the ear.

- Round the belly section, keeping it lower at the right and left side where it touches the legs.

- Try using CA glue to hold the head section together for shaping. Instead of cutting out a sanding shim for each piece, you can easily and quickly spot glue, sand, then break the pieces apart to sand the other edges. This is a wonderful time saver. Round the edges of the tacked head. Make the area next to the ear lower. Put a concave slope at the point where the muzzle meets the head right near the eye. If your piece comes apart while you are sanding, re-glue in a different area. You may have not used enough glue or glued at a point where the two pieces were not tightly joined. When you are pleased with the results, break apart the pieces by gently rapping on a hard surface. If the pieces don't come apart easily, you used too much glue. Use CA solvent in the seams first to loosen the glue. If it still won't come apart you will have to recut the seam on the pieces. Clean off any CA glue in your seams with an X-Acto knife. See page 45 for more information.

- Put a slight beveled edge on the pieces where the eye sections are located. This will add expression to your pup.

- Use a small brush to carefully apply white stain on the light wood up to the color break lines. After a few minutes, use a clean area on a rag to wipe from the dark wood toward the white piece. This will prevent any white stain from getting on the darker wood. Let dry overnight.

- Use clear gloss varnish on the eye to impart a life-like sparkle.

Materials

- 2" x 2" x 1" (51mm x 51mm x 25mm) black wood (ebony)

- 6" x 6" x 1" (152mm x 152mm x 25mm) dark wood (wengè, black walnut)

- 6" x 5" x 1" (152mm x 127mm x 25mm) medium wood (cherry)

- 11" x 8" x 1" (279mm x 203mm x 25mm) white wood (poplar)

- 3" x 3" x 1" (76mm x 76mm x 25mm) red wood (cocobolo)

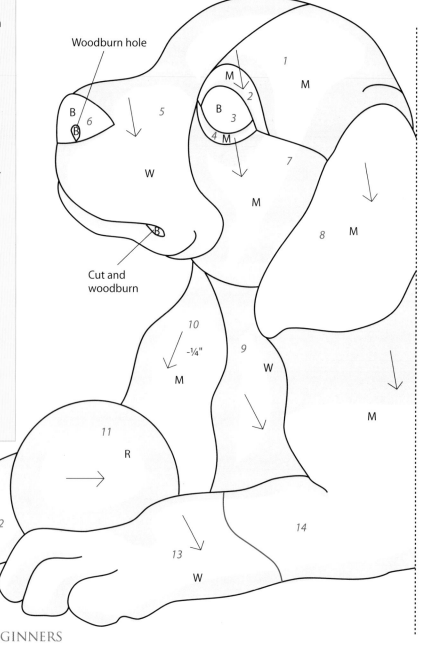

Woodburn hole

Cut and woodburn

Enlarge pattern 125% for actual size.

8

M

14

M

15

D

17   M

16

W

18

W

W
−¼"
20

M   19

M
−¼"

Enlarge pattern
125% for actual size.

LEGEND

→   Grain direction
B   Black or dark shade
D   Dark shade
M   Medium shade
W   White shade
R   Red shade
−¼   ¼" (6mm) sand down or thinner wood
——   Color breaks

LEVEL 1

Tortoise

Materials

- 1" x 1" x ½" (25mm x 25mm x 13mm) black wood (black ebony)
- 10" x 5" x 1" (254mm x 127mm x 25mm) dark wood (black walnut)
- 18" x 6" x 1" (457mm x 152mm x 25mm) light wood (ash)

Tips

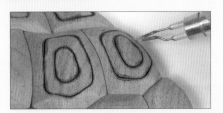

Woodburn smaller shapes inside each shell piece.

- I recommend a #5 blade for the outside of the shell and a #3 for all the inside cuts.

- Hand carve or use a rotary tool to add any carved details to the head and feet.

- Sand each shell piece with gem facets—sharp angles on the sides and a flat spot in the middle.

- Use a flat tip for filling in and shading large areas like the toenails. This can save you from cutting out each toenail from a darker wood and fitting them in place.

- Use the sanding mop on the shell to remove the excess burned edges of the lines.

- See further instruction in Lesson 12, Using Shims to Add a 3-D Effect, page 37.

LEGEND

→ Grain direction
B Black shade
D Dark shade
L Light shade
----- Shims
-¼ ¼" (6mm) sand down or thinner wood
——— Lines for woodburning

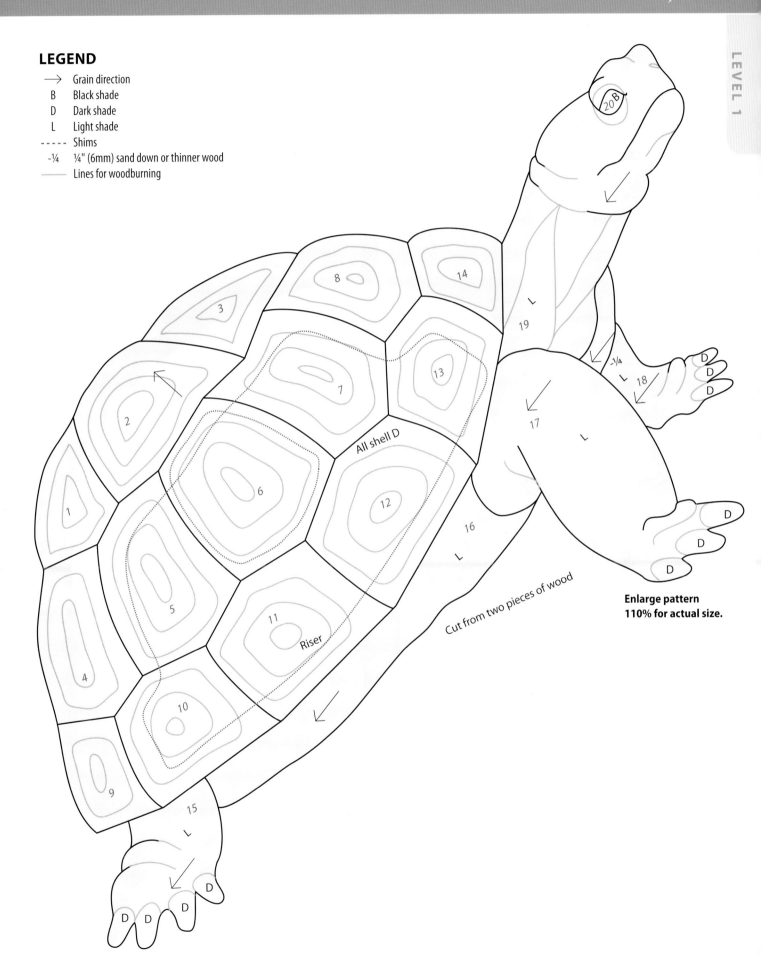

Enlarge pattern
110% for actual size.

LEVEL 1

Train Photo Frame

Materials

- 16" x 7" x 1" (406mm x 178mm x 25mm) dark wood (black walnut)
- 30" x 9" x 1" (762mm x 229mm x 25mm) white wood (poplar)

Tips

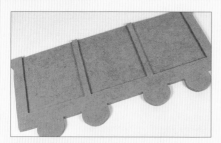

Cut out the backer boards by using double-stick tape and taping two boards together, rough side up. After you have cut out the set, take apart the two boards and only cut the top one with the pattern still attached. Cut the red lines for the photo holes. Glue the two pieces together using CA and wood glue.

- This is a fun simple project I designed for my little cousin Jake, a big fan of trains. Add overlay letters to personalize your photo frame for the little guy or girl you know.

- The train can be cut from several colors of wood or just one piece of wood and stained. I chose to use black walnut for the dark wood and a piece of poplar for all the other areas, which were stained green, red, and yellow—perfect for a child's room.

- The train and the car can be linked together with a chain for a unique touch.

- You can make several cars to attach to the train for a long photo gallery.

- There are a lot of straight cuts on this project. After you have cut them, run them over the flat drum sander to make them perfectly flat and straight.

- I put a coat of Danish dark walnut oil on my black walnut pieces.

Train Photo Frame

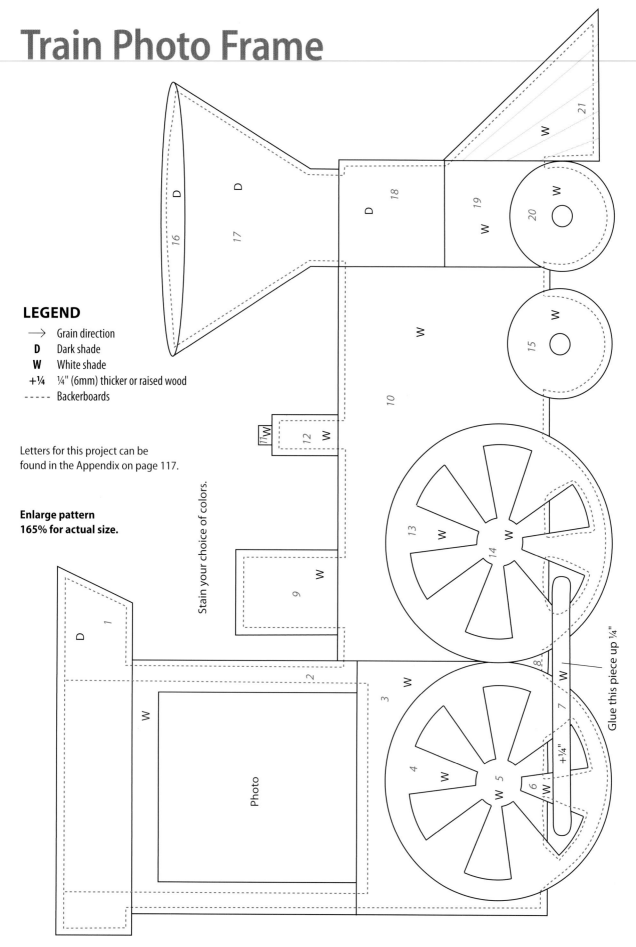

LEGEND

→   Grain direction
D   Dark shade
W   White shade
+¼   ¼" (6mm) thicker or raised wood
- - - -   Backerboards

Letters for this project can be
found in the Appendix on page 117.

**Enlarge pattern
165% for actual size.**

Stain your choice of colors.

Glue this piece up ¼"

Photo

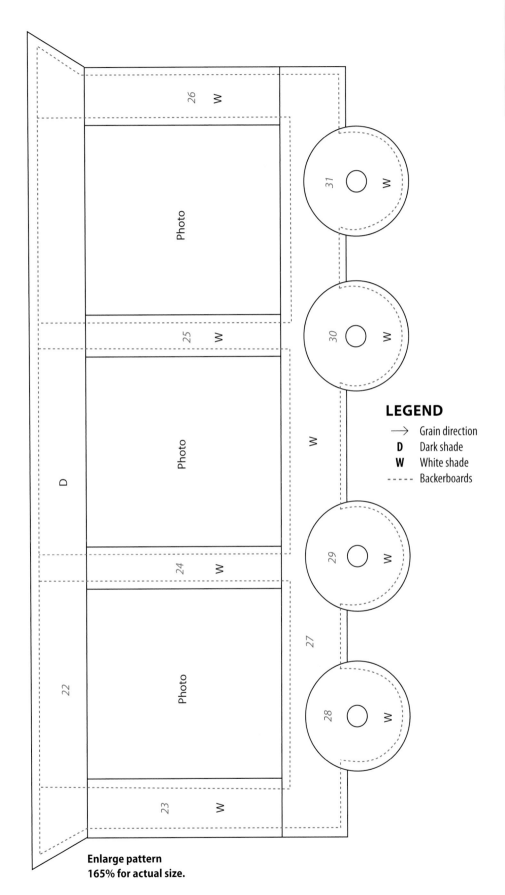

LEGEND

→ Grain direction
D Dark shade
W White shade
- - - - Backerboards

**Enlarge pattern
165% for actual size.**

LEVEL 2 STEP-BY-STEP PROJECT:
Horse

Because I started my art career sculpting animals from clay, I strive to bring a three-dimensional aspect to all my intarsia work. Sanding and shaping is very intimidating for most beginners. Some simply round all the edges of the pieces of a project, resulting in a fairly flat finished intarsia. Here, I will explain how to sand each piece for the greatest illusion of depth. Adding shims and creating shadows by deep sanding will make your project seem to pop out at you.

Materials

- 3" x 3" x ½" (76mm x 76mm x 13mm) black wood, eye (ebony)
- 24" x 8" x 1" (610mm x 203mm x 25mm) dark wood, mane (black walnut)
- 4" x 6" x 1" (102mm x 152mm x 25mm) medium-dark wood (dark section of cherry)
- 25" x 9" x 1" (635mm x 229mm x 25mm) medium wood, head and neck (cherry)

Enlarge pattern 135% for actual size.

LEGEND

→	Grain direction
B	Black shade
D	Dark shade
MD	Medium-dark shade
M	Medium shade
-¼	¼" (6mm) thinner wood
+½	½" (13mm) thicker wood or shim
-----	Shim

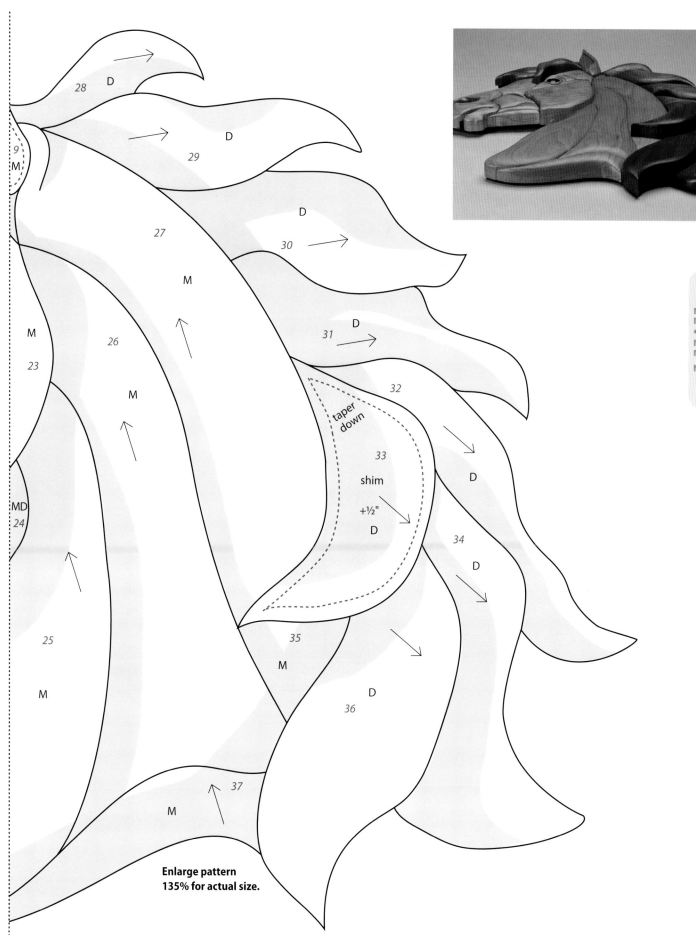

28 D

9
M

D
29

27

M

D
30

M
M
23

M
26

D
31

32

M

taper
down

33

shim

+½"

D

D

MD
24

M
25

D
34

D

35

M

M

D
36

D

37

M

**Enlarge pattern
135% for actual size.**

LEVEL 2

LEVEL 2 STEP-BY-STEP PROJECT: **HORSE**

1

Apply patterns: Make six copies of the pattern. Cut apart, spray the backs with adhesive, and stick to the shiny side of contact paper. Cut out each color and group together. Peel and stick to your boards. Trim down the wood into manageable pieces.

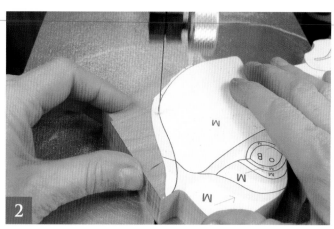

2

Begin to cut: Check your blade for squareness. I use a regular skip tooth #5 blade because it cuts thick wood very well. Beginners should use softer woods. Cut the outside lines of the large head and neck sections with the #5 blade.

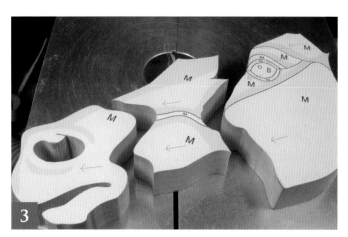

3

Cut the head: Use a #3 blade to separate large sections. Smaller blades make smaller kerfs—your piece will fit better. Drill a hole in the nostril and cut it out. Cut the nose (17)—that opens up pieces 14–16. Number the backs and lay them on your workboard.

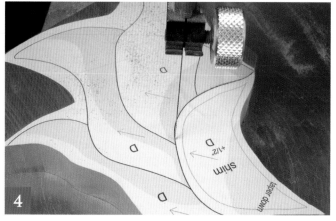

4

Cut the mane: Cut piece 33. This opens up 32, 34, and 36—in that order. Take care to cut all of the interior lines accurately. The outside lines can be cut in a more relaxed manner, as imprecision there won't affect fitting.

Tips

- For the best results from this tutorial you should use 1" (25mm)-thick wood. The thicker wood will make it easier to get more depth in your project.

- You can use a white wood for the mane and a lighter brown for the head and neck if you don't want a horse with the same colors I chose.

- Soft woods will be easiest to use for beginners.

- Try to find a piece of wood with an interesting flowing grain for the mane pieces.

- Always use the same board for areas that are the same color. Example: the head section and the neck section. If you used two different cherry boards the color may be slightly different and will look out of place when finished.

- Cut the thicker wood slowly so your blade doesn't bend and create slanted edges on the pieces.

5

Create the eye: Lay out the eye pattern on your ½" (13mm) ebony. Drill a hole for your white highlight. Insert and glue a white dowel before you cut out the eye. Trim the dowel, level the surface, and cut out the eye. Glue the eye to a shim. Round the eye on the drum sander, then finish with the sanding mop.

Complete cutting: Cut out the rest and assemble. Do the colors look good? Are there any flaws you didn't notice before? Are there any distracting sections? Now is the time to make any wood changes needed.

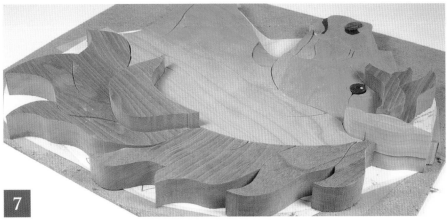

Add shims: Review lesson 12 for more pointers on shims. Look over your project and determine which areas will be highest or closest to you. On this project, pieces 8, 9, 13, and 33 are highest. We will shim those pieces up. This will give your project a 3-D effect.

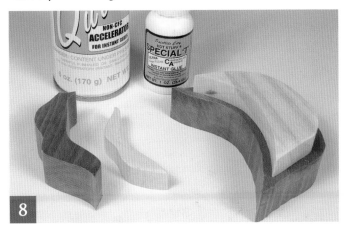

Cut mane shims: Cut the 2 shims for the mane sections (13, 33) from ½" (13mm)-thick scrap wood. Make sure the shims are smaller than the pieces and don't stick out. Glue the pieces to the shims and set back in place on the board.

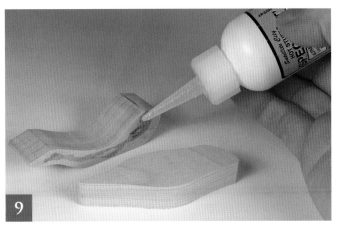

Add height to ear: To make 1½" (38mm)-thick wood for the ear (8, 9), use a band saw to cut a 1" (25mm) piece of the same wood in half. Glue to the 1" piece. Match the grain. The pieces must be flat. Line up the edges and CA glue the pieces. Sand the edges on an oscillating sander.

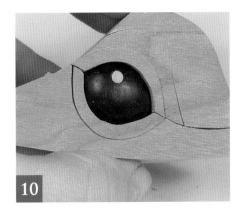

Fit the eye: Fit the eye with the surrounding pieces (1, 2, 4–6). Grasp together and hold up to the light. If you see gaps, the eye is slightly too big. Sand a little bit at a time where the wood touches to draw the pieces tighter.

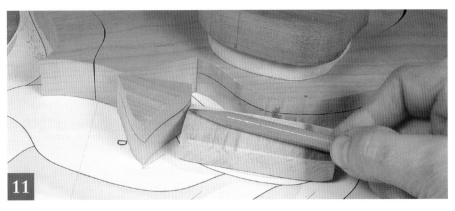

Mark shim level: Use a scrap piece of the shim to mark the shim level on all pieces surrounding shimmed areas. You must stay above this line when sanding or your shim will be exposed.

LEVEL 2 STEP-BY-STEP PROJECT: **HORSE**

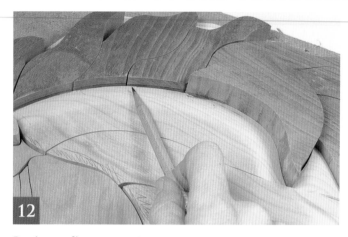

12

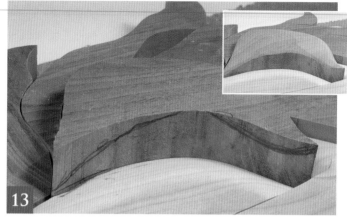

13

Begin sanding: Start with 27, the neck. Round the edges—do not cross the shim line. Sand 26, 35, and 37 to the line. Mark and sand a slope to the mane (pieces 28–31) at neck level (shown). Begin shaping the mane using the shaping guide.

Create slopes: Mark the highest shimmed piece (33). Put a flowing slope on it by tapering the end closest to the neck down to the neck level. When you add sloping curves to your pieces, you get more dimension to your piece.

14

Sand the mane:
By putting a sharp downward angle on each mane piece, it will make the adjacent piece appear higher. The deep contour allows shadows to form, which creates a three-dimensional quality. Be careful not to sand all the way to the bottom or expose shims.

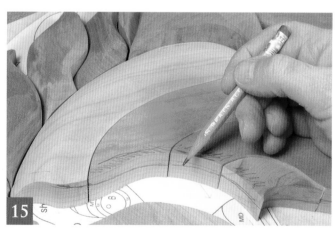

15

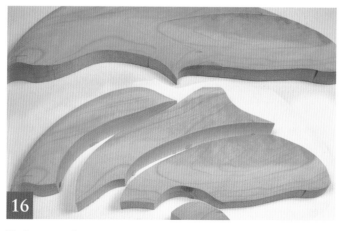

16

Contour the neck: Sand a sloped edge on 37. Mark and slope pieces 24–27 so they appear lower than the cheek (23).

Tack to sand: CA glue the neck area together to sand as one. Follow lessons 9 and 17 for more details. Mark and sand the entire neck section then break apart and sand the edges of each piece slightly.

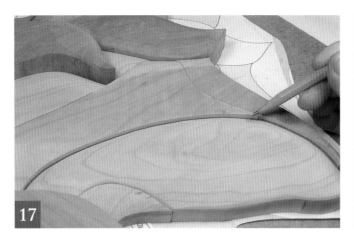

17

Continue sanding the neck: Sand each piece, replace it on the board next to the other pieces, and mark your level for the next piece. You want to get a curved look to each section with a nice consistent line in-between.

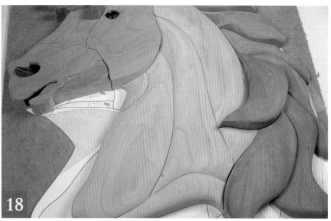

18

Evaluate the neck and mane: Lay out your neck and mane pieces on your workboard and check to make sure it is sanded to your satisfaction. Now move on to the head section.

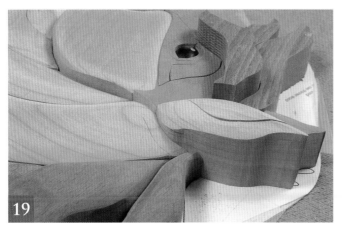

19

Sand the cheek: Sand the cheek section flat, just slightly rounding the edges. Round the ears, bringing the level at the neck almost even and tapering up to the tip of the ear. Remove the inside of the ear (8) and sand down about ¼" (6mm).

20

Sand piece 10: Sand the lowest piece (10). Mark your level next to the shimmed ear. Shape and set in place. Don't go below the red marked shim line.

Sand the forelock: Put the mane forelock pieces (11–13) in place and mark your sanding line. Be sure to mark the inside shim line on pieces 11 and 12 so you do not sand too low. Round the edges.

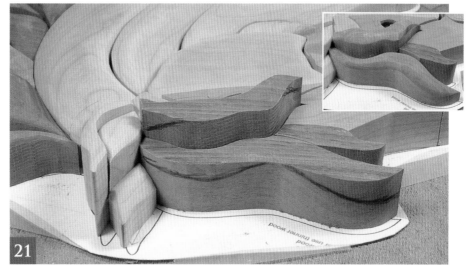

21

LEVEL 2 STEP-BY-STEP PROJECT: **HORSE**

Sand 6 and 7: Sand pieces 6 and 7 by rounding the edges. Each time you sand a piece and put it back in place, mark the piece next to it for a sanding level guide.

Continue rounding the eye sections: Use the oscillating sander or a rotary tool to get the inside angles. Replace often to check your levels in relation to the other pieces.

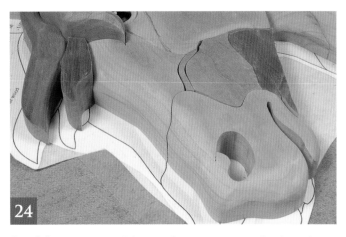

Sand the nose: Round the top of nose pieces 14 and 17 by tacking the two pieces together with a few drops of CA glue. This will give you a nice continuous contour on the side. Break apart after sanding.

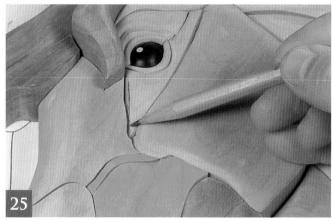

Round: Mark the edge of piece 14 where it meets 5. Round down to the line. Round forelock piece 12.

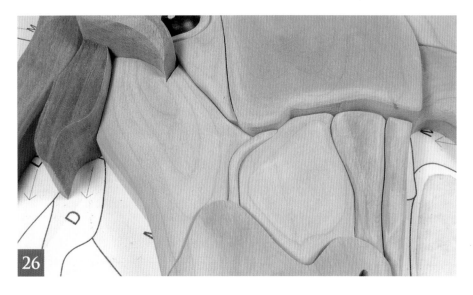

Shape: Shape 15, 16, 21, and 22, marking as you go.

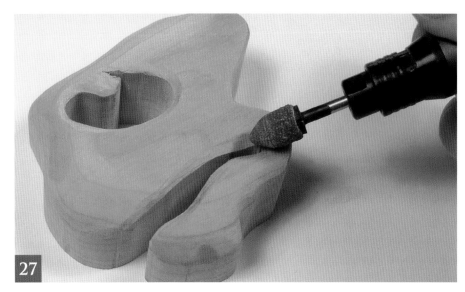

Shape the nostril: Round the edges of the nose piece 17. Use a rotary tool with a sanding sleeve (or burr of your choice) to round the nostril and inside of the mouth.

Check: Lay out all your pieces and check for fit. Recut or sand to fit if needed.

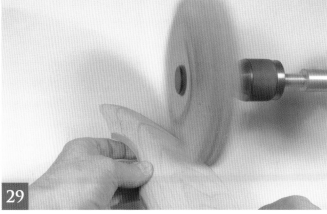

Sand with mop: Sand all of the pieces on the sanding mop. I use two mops: first a 150-grit and then a 220-grit. If you are using cherry wood, make sure your speed is slow or you will burn the wood.

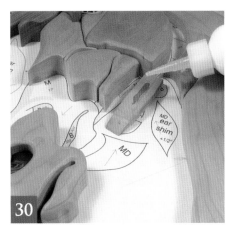

Glue the nose: I will CA glue most of the pieces without accelerator so I have more time to set the pieces together. Start with the nose section. Glue 14–22; press together and let set up about 5 minutes. Leave in place on your pattern.

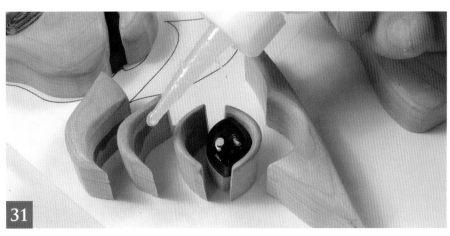

Glue the eye: Glue 1, 2, and 4–6 together and put in place. Leave the eye (3) in position but do not glue. We will add the glue after we varnish the entire piece. Glue pieces 7 and 23 together.

LEVEL 2 STEP-BY-STEP PROJECT: HORSE

LEVEL 2

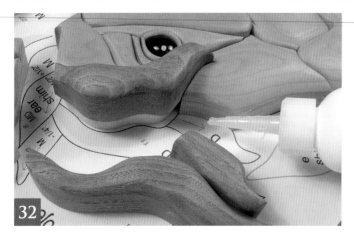

32

33

Complete gluing of the head: Glue the forelock pieces (11–13) in place and then the ears (8–10). Let the entire head section set up.

Glue the neck and mane: Glue the neck (24–27, 35, 37) while in place next to the head. Let the neck set up before moving onto the mane (28–34, 36). Start with the bottom (36) and work up. Glue quickly so you can adjust the pieces before the mane sets.

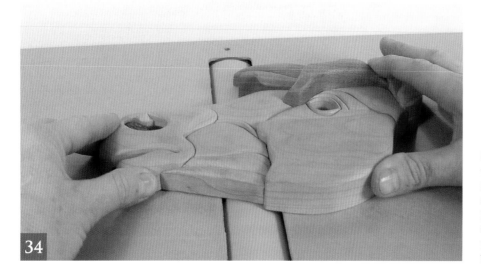

34

Flat sand: Flat sand the neck and head sections. Make sure all of the uneven pieces are flat and all of the glue globs or paper are removed from the backs.

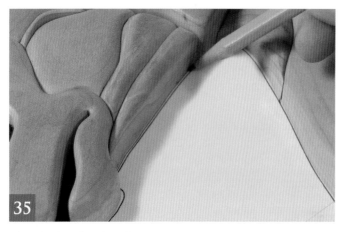

35

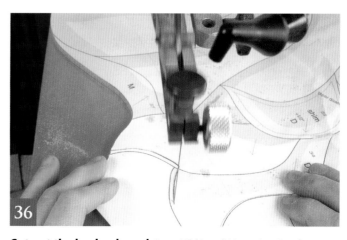

36

Glue the head and neck: CA glue the neck and head together and flat sand. Place the piece on the pattern backerboard and trace any lines that have shifted. Use the sanding mop to gently remove any pencil marks from the edges of the piece.

Cut out the backer board: I use ¼" (6mm) Masonite. Put the pattern on the rough side so the back will be smooth. Use a reverse-tooth blade and stay just inside the lines. You can tilt your saw and put a bevel on the edges if you like.

LEVEL 2

Paint the backer board: Spray paint the back side of the backer board for a professional-looking finish.

37

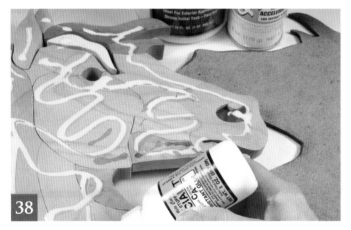

38

Glue the horse to the backer board: Spray the backer board with accelerator and put CA and wood glue on the horse. Center the board and attach it. Hold in place for a minute, then flip the piece over and apply pressure to make sure the glue adheres.

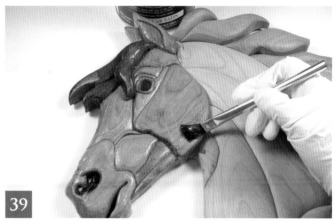

39

Apply gel varnish: Use clear gel varnish. Brush a thick coat on just the head and wipe off the excess with a rag. You don't want to use gel varnish on too large an area at once because it will dry and be hard to wipe off.

Complete the project: Use an air gun or canned air to blow out the gel from the crevices. Wipe the project clean as you go. Let dry overnight. Wipe down with a gel varnish–saturated rag, wipe clean, and let dry overnight. Glue in the clear glossed–eye. Attach a mirror style hanger.

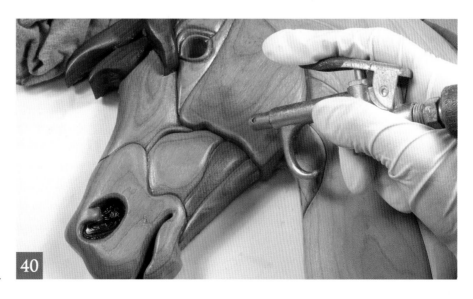

40

Frog

LEVEL 2

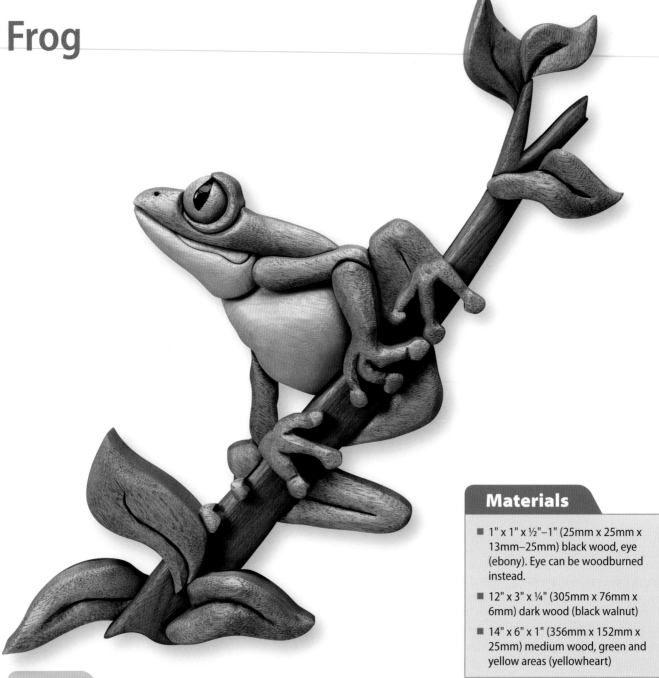

Materials

- 1" x 1" x ½"–1" (25mm x 25mm x 13mm–25mm) black wood, eye (ebony). Eye can be woodburned instead.
- 12" x 3" x ¼" (305mm x 76mm x 6mm) dark wood (black walnut)
- 14" x 6" x 1" (356mm x 152mm x 25mm) medium wood, green and yellow areas (yellowheart)

Tips

- This project was out from one piece of yellowheart and one piece of walnut. The green sections are stained yellowheart pieces.

- Pieces 9, 12, 14, 18, and 19 are overlays and will be glued on top of the branch.

- Shape the branch with a slight bevel on the edges. Keep the middle area flat. The branch will only be about ½" (13mm) thick.

- Shape the overlay feet using a small die grinder or Dremel tool. The feet overlays will only be about ½" thick when you are done.

- Lightly stain the leaves and green sections of the frog using your stain or dye of choice and let dry overnight. You could also use lignum vitae or other green wood for those parts.

- Use snakewood or lacewood for an interesting mottled frog skin effect.

- Woodburn bark, leaf, and frog skin detail if desired.

- Use a traditional backer board, or glue to an oval or square backer board with a frame.

- Try making the project without overlays—it will be a good exercise in fitting.

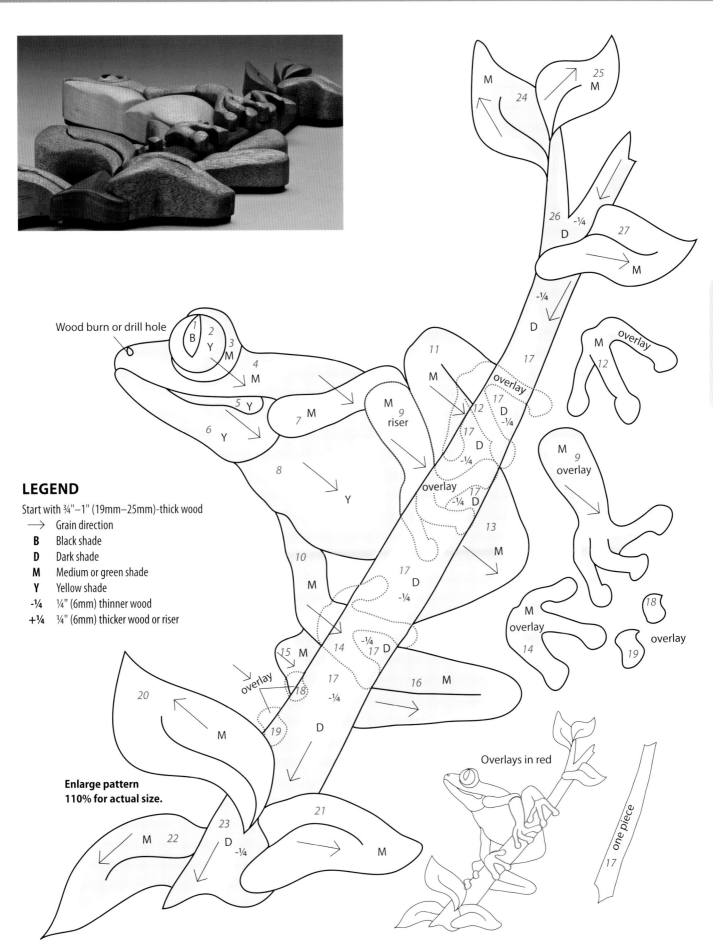

Wood burn or drill hole

25
24
M
M
26 -¼
D
27
M
-¼
D
17

11
M
M 9
riser
overlay
17
D
-¼
12
17
D
overlay
17
D
-¼
13
M

12
M overlay

M 9
overlay

1
2
B
Y
3
M
4
M
5 Y
7 M
6 Y
8
Y

LEGEND

Start with ¾"–1" (19mm–25mm)-thick wood

→ Grain direction
B Black shade
D Dark shade
M Medium or green shade
Y Yellow shade
-¼ ¼" (6mm) thinner wood
+¼ ¼" (6mm) thicker wood or riser

10
M
17
D
-¼
M

18
M overlay
14
19 overlay

15 M
14
-¼
17 D
16 M

overlay
18
17
-¼

20
M
19
D

Enlarge pattern 110% for actual size.

Overlays in red

one piece
17

22 M
23
D -¼
21
M

LEVEL 2

Lighthouse

Materials

- 2" x 2" x 1" (51mm x 51mm x 25mm) black wood (ebony)
- 13" x 7" x 1" (330mm x 178mm x 25mm) dark wood (wengè)
- 5" x 5" x 1" (127mm x 127mm x 25mm) medium-dark wood (black walnut)
- 8" x 6" x ½" (203mm x 152mm x 13mm) medium-light wood (curly maple)
- 6" x 5" x 1" (152mm x 127mm x 25mm) red wood (bloodwood)
- 11" x 10" x ¼" (279mm x 254mm x 6mm) light wood (birch)
- 6" x 4" x 1" (152mm x 102mm x 25mm) white wood (poplar)

Tips

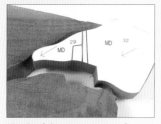

Think of the two pieces of medium dark hills (29 and 32) behind the lighthouse as one continuing piece. Lay the patterns out on your board next to each other as if the lighthouse wasn't there. In your finished piece it will look much better than grains that don't quite match.

Save all of the waste window cutouts as you scroll. You can sand them down and use them as risers for your ½" (13mm) ebony windows.

- I used a piece of birch for the sky; it had some interesting brown specks in it, but not enough to make it distracting.

- I chose a beautiful piece of curly maple for the sea. It had some very attractive grain patterns that suit this project very well. Although the material list only calls for 8" x 6" (203mm x 152mm) of wood you will need at least an entire board to pick the perfect grain.

- The foreground hill is a piece of cherry with some interesting grain patterns.

- Lay out pieces 26 and 27 next to each other.

- Sand the lighthouse sections to a sharp angle towards the middle section.

- Leave the lighthouse sections unglued but in place as you glue the other sections together. This will ensure they will fit in place.

LEVEL 2

LEVEL 2

LEGEND

→   Grain direction
B   Black or dark shade
D   Dark shade
MD   Medium-dark shade
M   Medium shade
ML   Medium-light shade
R   Red shade
W   White shade
-¼   ¼" (6mm) sand down or thinner wood
+¼   ¼" (6mm) thicker wood or riser

**Enlarge pattern
145% for actual size.**

Sunflower

Materials

LEVEL 2

- 3" x 10" x ¼" (76mm x 254mm x 6mm) dark wood (wengè)
- 3" x 3" x ¼" (76mm x 76mm x 6mm) medium-dark wood (mahogany)
- 8" x 6" x ¾" (203mm x 152mm x 19mm) medium wood (green poplar)
- 8" x 5" x 1" (203mm x 127mm x 25mm) red wood (cherry)
- 8" x 8" x 1" (203mm x 203mm x 25mm) yellow wood (yellowheart)
- 40" (1016mm) of ⅜" (10mm) walnut dowel

Tips

Mark the petals down ½" (13mm) all around the inside and about 1" (25mm) in on the top around the inside circle. Do not go below the stem or the leaves. Sand a slope on each petal between the lines.

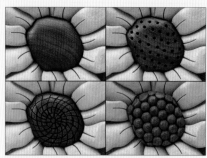

You can make the center plain, drilled, woodburned, or with dowels. The dowel center is the most work, but I think it is also the most interesting of the four choices.

- Slope the edges of piece 28 toward the back of the project.

- Pay special attention to the color break on the pot (pieces 26 and 27). Taper the right and left edges of the pot to make it appear round. Sand down under the rim about ¼" (6mm) to make the rim seem higher.

- Round the very edges of the dirt and back of the pot; these are only about ½" (13mm) thick. Taper the pot pieces slightly below the dirt pieces.

- Take off more wood at the top of the leaves where they fit under the petals. Make each leaf slope from the middle vein line to the sides. Make concave slopes on the leaves to make them look wrinkled. You can use a rotary tool or an oscillating sander with a ½" (13mm) sleeve as I did.

- To glue the sunflower together, first use CA glue to attach 26, 27, and 28 to each other. Next, glue together the rim (24 and 25), leaves (16, 18, and 23), stem (14), dirt (15, 17, 19–22), and two petals (7 and 8). Then, fit in the rest of the petals and glue in one at a time, starting at one side and working your way around the circle.

- To make the center, start by tracing a new pattern for the center from the glued petals. You need to do this instead of using the one from the pattern because when you cut apart the petals, the kerf changed the size and made it slightly smaller. Make a ¼" (6mm) plywood shim to fit exactly. You can woodburn the center, drill holes in it, leave it plain, or add dowel rods. I recommend ⅜" (10mm) dowels, cut into 1" (25mm) pieces. Round the tops and glue to the riser. Sand and trim the edges to fit the riser.

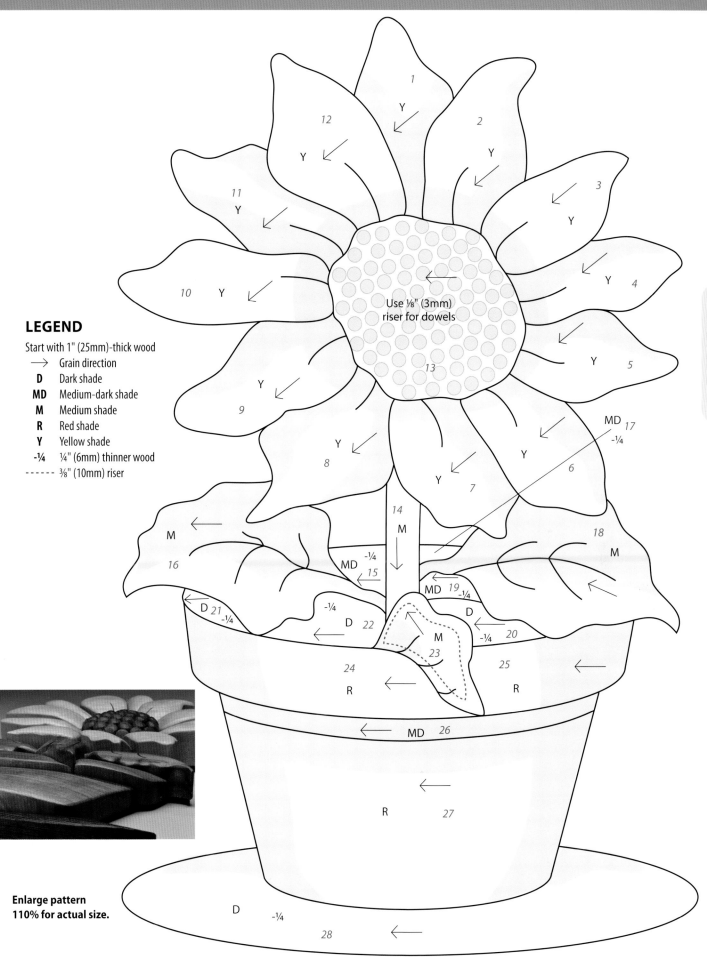

LEGEND

Start with 1" (25mm)-thick wood
- → Grain direction
- **D** Dark shade
- **MD** Medium-dark shade
- **M** Medium shade
- **R** Red shade
- **Y** Yellow shade
- **-¼** ¼" (6mm) thinner wood
- - - - - - ⅜" (10mm) riser

Use ⅛" (3mm) riser for dowels

Enlarge pattern 110% for actual size.

Cowboy Boot Clock

Materials

- 13" x 10" x ⅜" (330mm x 254mm x 10mm) white wood (poplar)
- 13" x 10" x ¾" (330mm x 254mm x 19mm) medium wood (cherry or cedar)
- 11" x 13" x 1" (279mm x 330mm x 25mm) dark wood (black walnut)

Tips

- Make sure your wood is flat, and use double-stick carpet tape to attach the white and medium woods on top of each other for stack-cutting.

- Use a #5 standard blade to cut the outside lines of the stacked boots. Cut down the center of the boot and cut out the clock circle. Cut the boot into smaller sections, but do not cut out the inlay sections. Cut out the heel and bottom of the boot.

- Change your blade to a #3 to cut the boot inlay sections. You will not have to drill any holes because of the way the pattern is designed. Cut slowly and make your turns carefully. Do not back up if you go off the line—just ease back onto the line.

- CA glue the inlay sections together, making sure they are lined back up perfectly.

- Taper the heel back to the left. Round the sole and taper the edges to match the heel and toe of the boot. If you have a cowboy boot, get it out—it will help you visualize how to shape it.

- Use a die grinder with a burr to carve around the lines of the inlays and boot seams. Round all the edges slightly.

- Carve the inlays with some concave areas to simulate real leather tooling.

- If your clock insert does not fit in the hole, sand the inside circle with the oscillating sander to make it fit.

- Woodburn the stitching on the boot and sand lightly with a mop sander.

- If you want to create a free-standing desk clock, cut the backer board out of 1" (25mm) cherry. You can also cut another boot using a reversed pattern without the clock insert circle.

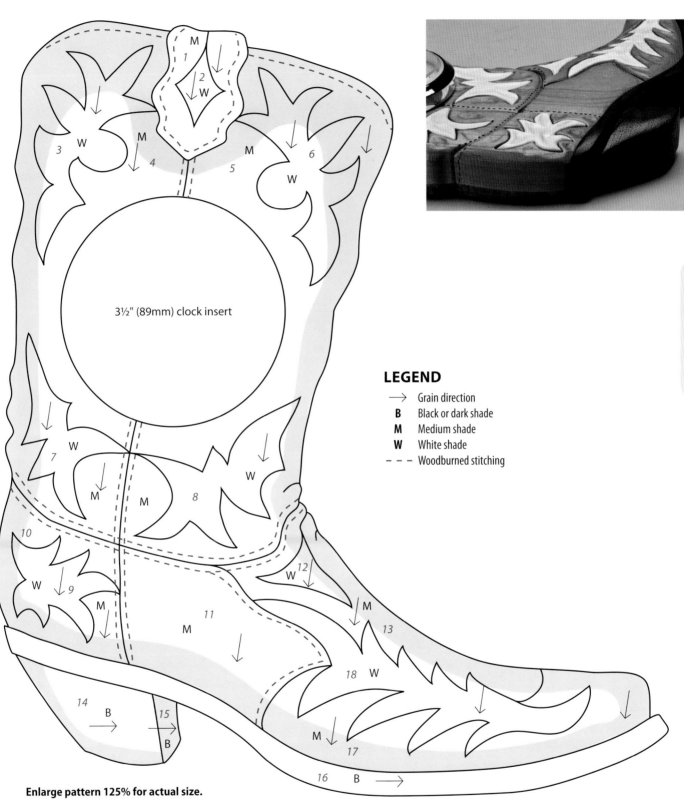

3½" (89mm) clock insert

LEGEND

$\longrightarrow$ Grain direction

B   Black or dark shade

M   Medium shade

W   White shade

– – –   Woodburned stitching

Enlarge pattern 125% for actual size.

LEVEL 2

LEVEL 3 STEP-BY-STEP PROJECT:
Girl with Boots

This step-by-step project will bring together all of the previous lessons. There are complex fitting areas and fine carving detail on the face. There are also several tiny pieces in the eye area. Remember, you can always change the patterns or use different methods to create your intarsia. Don't be boxed in by thinking you can only use the steps outlined in this book.

LEVEL 3

Materials

- 21" x 5" x ⅜" (533mm x 127mm x 10mm) dark wood, ground (wengè)
- 3" x 6" x 1¼" (76mm x 152mm x 32mm) dark wood, hair (black walnut)
- 7" x 8" x 1" (178mm x 203mm x 25mm) medium wood, pants (beech)
- 9" x 7" x 1" (229mm x 178mm x 25mm) red wood, shirt (bloodwood)
- 12" x 8" x 1" (305mm x 203mm x 25mm) white wood, skin (aspen)
- 13" x 8" x 1" (330mm x 203mm x 25mm) yellow wood, hat and boots (yellowheart)
- 23" x 18" x ¼" (584mm x 457mm x 6mm) backer board

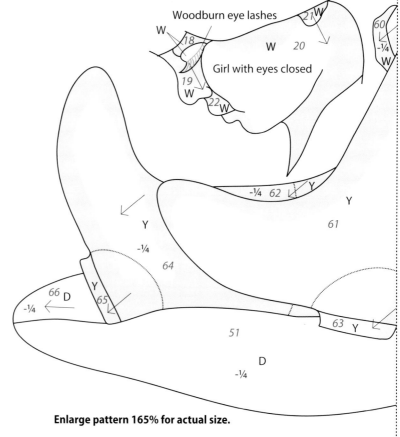

Woodburn eye lashes

Girl with eyes closed

Enlarge pattern 165% for actual size.

LEGEND

→	Grain direction
D	Dark shade
M	Medium shade
R	Red shade
W	White shade
Y	Yellow shade
-¼	¼" (6mm) thinner wood
+¼	¼" (6mm) thicker wood or riser
- - - -	Wood burn lines
- - - -	Shims

Enlarge pattern 165% for actual size.

LEVEL 3

LEVEL 3 STEP-BY-STEP PROJECT: **GIRL WITH BOOTS**

1

Apply patterns: Make seven copies of the pattern. Cut apart, spray the backs with adhesive, and stick onto the shiny side of contact paper. Cut out the patterns and place in groups by color. Attach patterns to wood. Trim down the wood into manageable pieces.

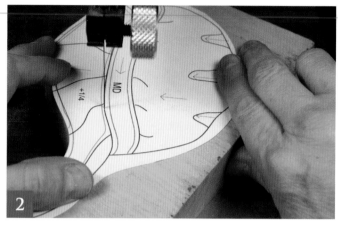

2

Cut: Cut out all of the pieces. When you cut the base (45, 51, and 66), cut out only the outside lines of the ground pieces. Do not cut the lines where the girl meets the ground. You will retrace the lines later for a tight fit.

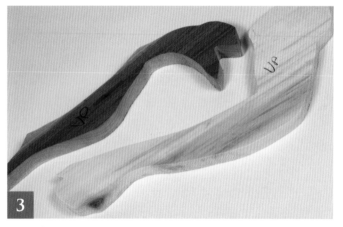

3

Cut shims: Cut out the shims for the hat brim (7–11), hair (29 and 30), and the arm (34) from ⅜"- or ½"- (10mm- or 13mm-) thick scrap wood. Mark the top side.

4

Check for fit: Lay out the pieces and check for fit, especially where two colors meet. Recut or sand any edges that have a bowed or slanted edge. The area where the fingers (34, 58) fit into the boot (59, 61) may need to be fitted.

Tips

Try substituting a closed eye or cutting it from one piece of wood and staining the pieces. You can also woodburn the eye details instead of cutting out the small pieces.

- Another way to make this project simpler is to use soft woods, which are easier to cut, and do not use any risers. You will not have as much 3-D effect, but you will still have a beautiful project.

- By cutting larger sections of your project—like the shirt, hat, and boots—from one piece of wood, your pieces will fit together easier.

- Check your blade on both sides to make sure it is square to the table.

- I use a #5 blade for the outside lines and switch to a #3 blade to cut apart each large section. If you are

using thick hard wood, you should stick to the #5 or the thinner blade will bend easily.

- Instead of cutting two separate shims for the hat and hair, try cutting them from one piece of wood.

- This project has a very fluid layout, which means the pieces will shift when one side is slightly moved, resulting in pieces that could be misaligned easily. Cut carefully and use silicon glue. Be sure to keep all of the tacked sections pressed up next to each other in place as you are gluing. This will ensure that your larger sections will fit later. See Lesson 4 for silicone gluing tips.

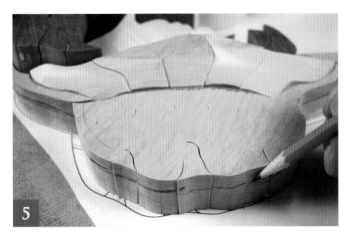

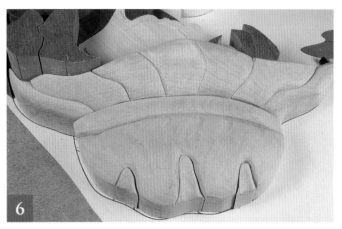

Mark the shim levels: Mark all of the shim levels on surrounding pieces next to the arm shim and hat shim pieces. Do not sand down past this line. Start sanding with the hat. Remember to mark, sand, replace, and repeat.

Shape: Mark the higher shimmed pieces and sand them down so they flow into the lower level. Keep the middle of the brim high and slope down on each side. Mark and round the band and cap sections (4 and 5).

Begin to sand: Use CA glue to tack 4 and 5; sand. Break apart, and sand the band edges. Sand the cap section lower next to the band. Sand the edges of each brim section (6–12). Sand one piece, replace it next to the others, and mark your level for the next piece.

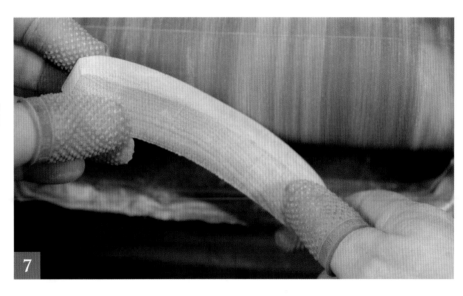

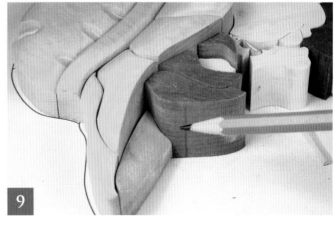

Add wrinkles to cap: Use the oscillating sander or a rotary tool to add the wrinkles in the cap. Sand the top three wrinkles by putting a slope in the middle of each one.

Sand piece 13: Mark the shim level on piece 13 and sand.

LEVEL 3

LEVEL 3 STEP-BY-STEP PROJECT: **GIRL WITH BOOTS**

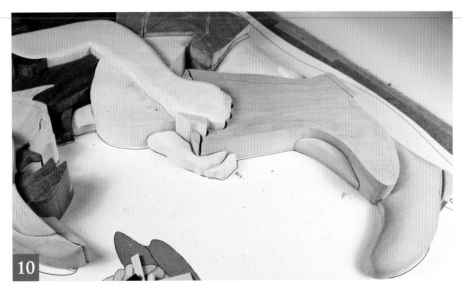

Sand the lowest pieces: Mark 23, 24, and 25 and sand down to about ⅜" or ½" (10mm or 13mm). Round the edges of the arm (25). Let the sleeve (23, 24) stay a bit higher than the arm piece. Sand the back hand pieces (57, 60). Sand the back boot (62, 64, 65) and back leg (53) and pant (52) sections. Don't go below the line you marked at the bottom of the legs that shows the lower height of the ground piece (51).

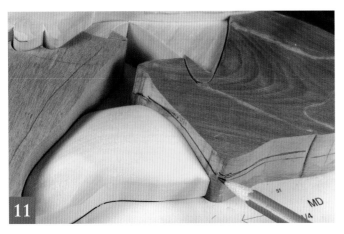

Round piece 53: Round the leg section (53), and then use it as a guide to mark the higher pants piece (52).

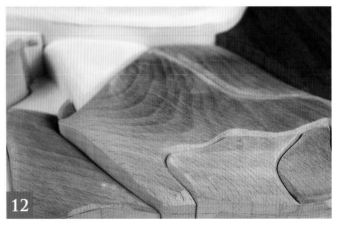

Sand the pants: Use CA glue to tack the pants sections (43, 44, 46, and 47) together and sand as one. Break apart and sand the edges slightly.

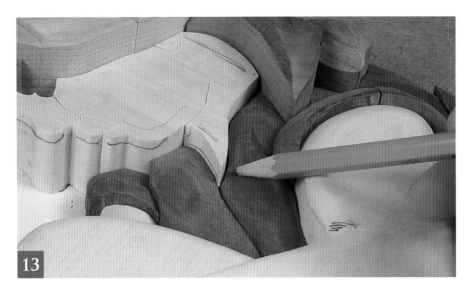

Sand the chest: Sand pieces 26 and 27, mark, and replace. Watch your shim lines so you don't go below them.

14

Sand the leg: Sand down piece 55 even with leg piece 48.

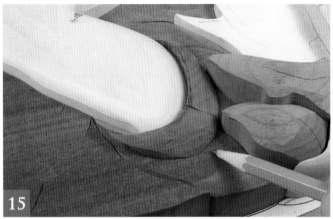

15

Sand the sleeves: Sand sections 33 and 50 to flow down to the lower level (31 and 32).

Sand the hair and shirt: Sand the hair (29, 30) to go under the hat and above the shoulder. Mark the sides of the shirt and the inside shim marks next to the arm (34). Round the shirt sections along the back. Sand sharply down at the top of each shirt piece so the fold on top rolls over the lower fold.

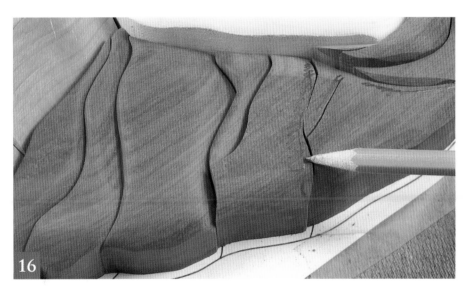

16

Sand the knee: Mark the knee and round slightly.

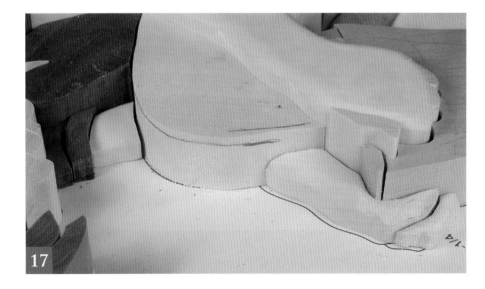

17

LEVEL 3

LEVEL 3 STEP-BY-STEP PROJECT: **GIRL WITH BOOTS**

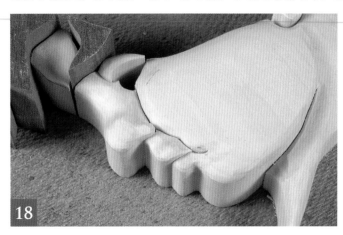

Sand the face: Sanding the face sections (16, 18–22) will require using a rotary tool or die grinder. A fine tapered sanding sleeve works very well to shape the mouth and face pieces. Use the close-up side photos to help with the sanding.

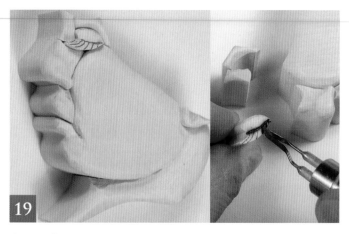

Create the eye: Glue the black eye piece to the small white eye piece and shape. There is a lot of small detail sanding with the eye. If you prefer a simpler face, use the closed eye version and woodburn the eye lash.

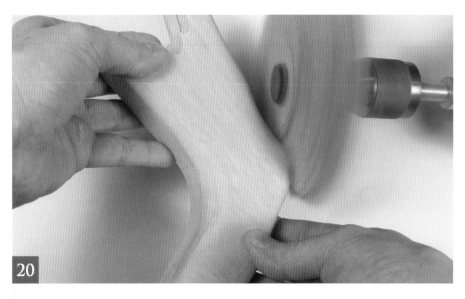

Sand with mop: Sand the bangs and forehead, then lay out all of the pieces and check for areas that need to be sanded a bit more. Check for sharp edges. Sand all of the pieces on the sanding mop. The tiny pieces will have to be hand sanded.

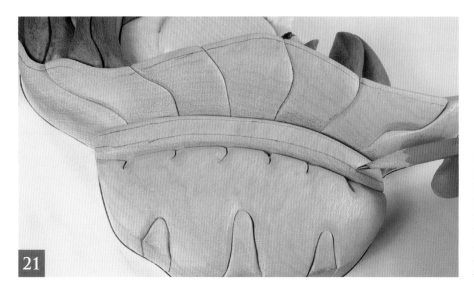

Mark the details: Mark a light pencil line on all of the pieces where the stitching will be— the boots (61, 62, and 64), hat (5–13), and pants (43, 44, 46, 47, 49, and 52).

LEVEL 3

Woodburn the details: Woodburn the stitching details on the boots, hat, and pants. Woodburn eyelash detail to the cheek below the eye (20). Use the sanding mop to soften the burned lines and remove the pencil lines.

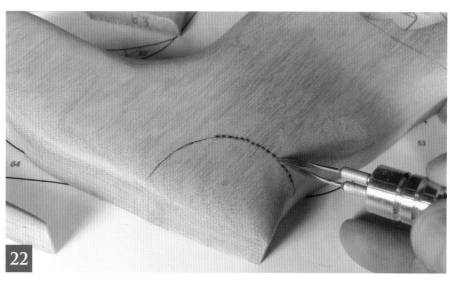

Glue the hat: We will use both CA and silicone glue on this project. Start by gluing pieces 7–11 together—place them on top of your pattern and next to piece 5. This will ensure you are gluing them in the right position.

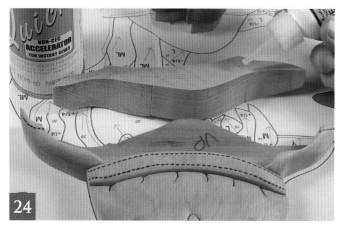

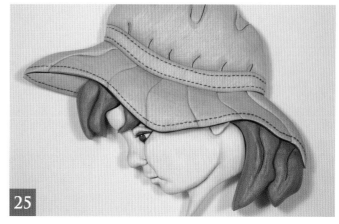

Complete gluing the hat: Glue the section you just glued to the shim. Put pieces 6 and 12 in place to keep the center section straight. Use CA glue to attach the center section to the band (5). Glue the rest of the hat together.

Glue the face: Use CA glue to attach the small face pieces and hair sections together. Glue the boots (59 and 61–65) and bangs sections (14–17), too.

LEVEL 3 STEP-BY-STEP PROJECT: **GIRL WITH BOOTS**

26

Use silicon glue: Place a few dots of silicone between the body and face pieces (18–42, 55, 56) and lay them out in place. (See information on page 20.) Also tack the pants and legs (43, 44, 46–49, 52, 53). Let dry overnight.

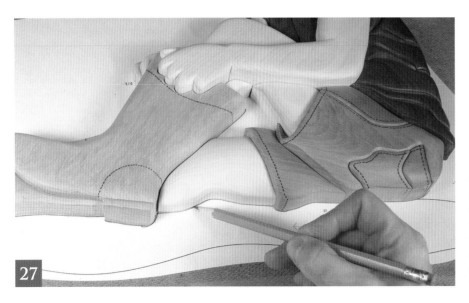

27

Trace the backer board: Lay out the tacked project onto the pattern taped to the board. Trace the outline of the girl along the bottom on the ground piece.

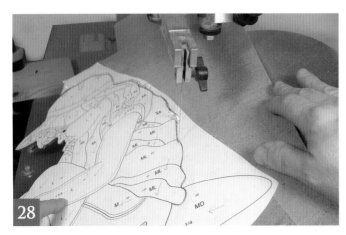

28

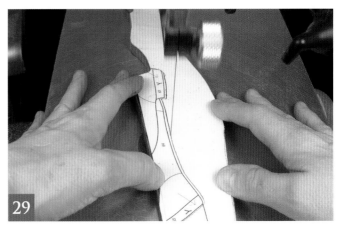

29

Cut out the backer board: Use a reverse-tooth blade for a clean cut and stay just inside the lines. You can tilt your saw and put a bevel on the backer if you wish. Spray paint the back for a professional-looking finish.

Cut out the ground: Cut out and peel off the bottom ground section of the backerboard pattern where you traced the outline of the girl. Use this as a guide to cut the top part of the ground pieces. Cut apart the ground pieces. CA glue the end pieces. Sand and fit.

LEVEL 3

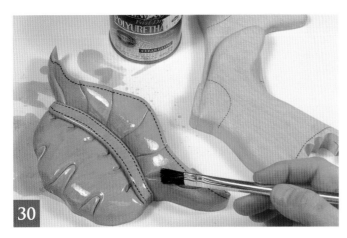

30

Apply brush-on finish: Use high clear gloss on just the hat and boots. The high shine will cause these pieces to have the appearance of vinyl—a nice contrast to the satin finish of the rest of the piece. Also paint the eye.

31

Apply spray finish: Spray the other pieces of the project with several coats of clear satin polyurethane. Let dry overnight.

Glue the girl to the backer board: Spray the backer board with accelerator. Put wood and CA glue all over the ground piece (51). Leave the other pieces in place. Glue the boots next (61–65), then the pants (43, 44, 46–49, 52, 53), then the body and head (18–42, 55, and 56).

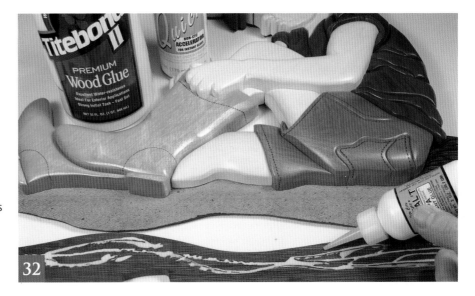

32

LEVEL 3

Complete the project: Glue the hat (1–13) and bangs (14–17) to the board. Trim any areas where the backer board shows from the front and touch up the edges with paint. Put a clear gloss on the eye. Attach a mirror-style hanger.

33

Lily Cross

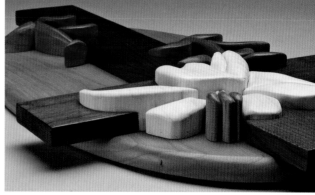

Tips

Mark and round the stems and leaves. Make the stems lower at the cross so they look like they are going behind the cross. Shape each leaf.

- The cross and lily are overlays on top of the oval backboard.

- Use shims to raise the two highest leaves (pieces 20 and 23) about ⅛" (3mm).

- Round the edges of the oval backer board using a router or the sanding drum. Flat sand the bottom surface.

- Sand the cross pieces, keeping the edges sharp.

- If you want to keep the lily from turning brown, use white stain on the lily pieces. I also used walnut oil on the cross sections in order to keep the dark wood very dark.

Materials

- 15" x 6" x ½" (381mm x 152mm x 13mm) dark wood (black walnut)

- 5" x 10" x ¾" (127mm x 254mm x 19mm) medium wood (mahogany)

- 2" x 2" x 1" (51mm x 51mm x 25mm) medium wood (beech)

- 16" x 10" x ½" (406mm x 254mm x 13mm) light wood, oval (cherry)

- 2" x 2" x 1" (51mm x 51mm x 25mm) light wood (sycamore)

- 8" x 7" x 1" (203mm x 178mm x 25mm) white wood (poplar)

LEVEL 3

LEGEND

→ Grain direction
D Dark shade
M Medium shade
L Light shade
W White shade
-¼ ¼" (6mm) thinner wood
── Backer board

5
W 6
7
W
-¼
1 D
L
W
2
W 3 4 10
M
W
M
M
15
9 L
D -¼
L 8
W
16
20
14 W
M
17
19 M
W W
-¼
22 D
W 11
21
23 M
24 M
M
-¼ 18
D-¼
W 12
25
M 26
D
13
-¼
L
29
D
-¼
27
-¼
28
M
31 M
M
33 M
30
M 32

Cut oval out of
½" stock in one
piece and use as
backerboard

**Enlarge pattern
150% for actual size.**

LEVEL 3

Raccoon

LEVEL 3

Materials

- 2" x 3" x ½" (152mm x 19mm x 381mm) black (ebony)

- 5" x 10" x 1" (127mm x 254mm x 25mm) dark wood (wengè)

- 16" x 8" x 1" (406mm x 203mm x 25mm) medium-dark wood (black walnut)

- 12" x 5" x 1" (305mm x 127mm x 25mm) medium wood (cherry)

- 15" x 6" x ¾" (381mm x 152mm x 19mm) red wood (bloodwood)

- 7" x 5" x 1" (178mm x 127mm x 25mm) white wood (poplar)

- 15" x 6" x ¾" (381mm x 152mm x 19mm) yellow wood (osage orange)

LEVEL 3

Tips

Tape a scrap piece of wood to the board as a stop so you can place the branch back into the exact position after you have applied the glue.

- Pay special attention to the area around the eyes when fitting.

- Cut a ⅜" (10mm) riser for the nose section (pieces 31–34). Use a riser for the eye if needed.

- Make sure all of the pieces flow into each other and there are no sharp edges between pieces.

- Use the oscillating sander to sand the inside curves of the ear pieces (16 and 23).

- You can treat the tail as a color break and make it one smooth piece, or you can add deep texture to each separate piece for an eye-catching effect. For more on deep texturing, see Lesson 16 (page 43).

- Use the white stain on your white pieces to keep them from turning brown if you wish.

- Glue the head in one section and fit it to the body and hanging arm. Recut your seams if your fit is off. Leave the hand (pieces 6 and 7) unglued to the arm, as this will be part of the branch section. CA glue the leaves together in sections, then glue to the branch and hand pieces.

Raccoon

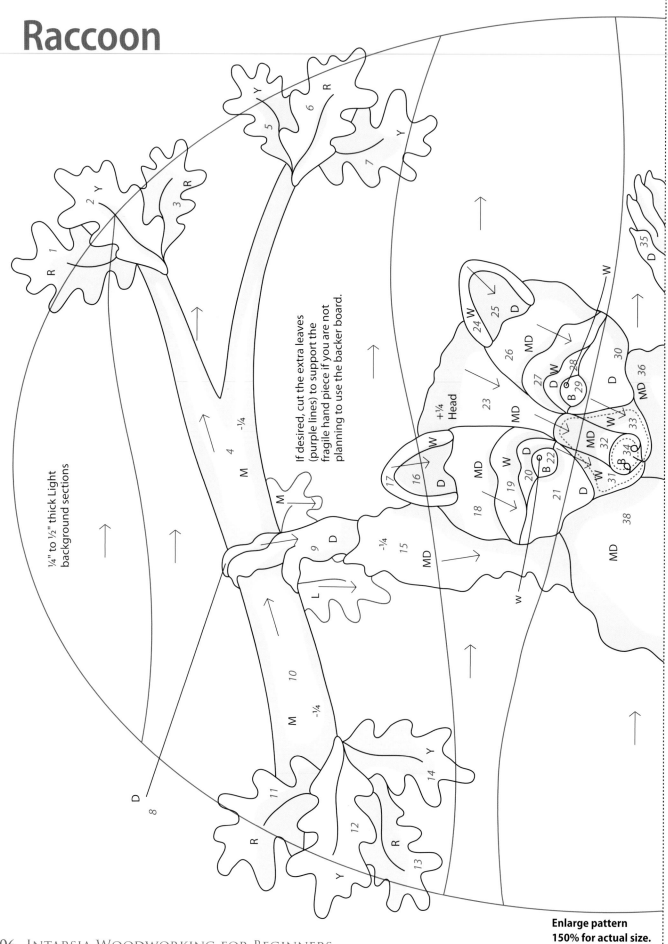

¼" to ½" thick Light background sections

If desired, cut the extra leaves (purple lines) to support the fragile hand piece if you are not planning to use the backer board.

LEVEL 3

Enlarge pattern 150% for actual size.

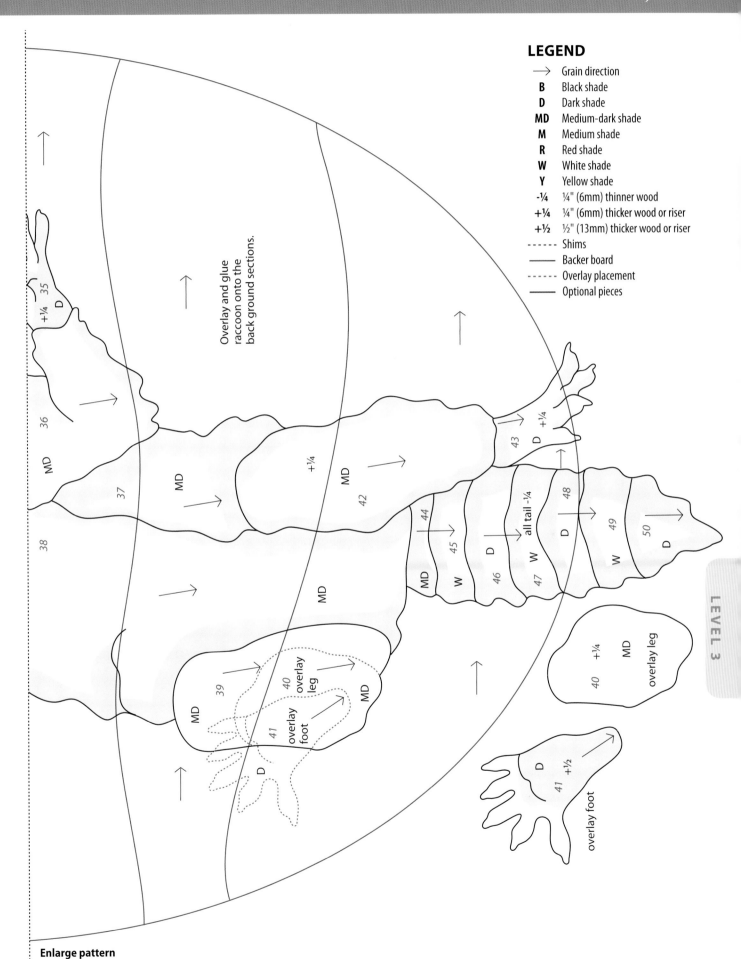

LEGEND

→	Grain direction
B	Black shade
D	Dark shade
MD	Medium-dark shade
M	Medium shade
R	Red shade
W	White shade
Y	Yellow shade
-¼	¼" (6mm) thinner wood
+¼	¼" (6mm) thicker wood or riser
+½	½" (13mm) thicker wood or riser
- - - - -	Shims
———	Backer board
- - - - -	Overlay placement
———	Optional pieces

Overlay and glue raccoon onto the back ground sections.

LEVEL 3

**Enlarge pattern
150% for actual size.**

Birdfeeder

Tips

Mark and sand the bottom piece (3) with a downward slope to the left. Sand the edges with sharp angles going back and away.

Sand the lower right pieces with a slant to the right. Mark and sand the large piece 11 with a sharp slant. It is highest from the left side going down to the left.

Make sure piece 12 is below bottom pieces 2 and 4.

- Beginners should cut the feeder from one piece of cedar and disregard the grain direction arrows. This will make fitting much easier.

- This is a good project to practice sanding for depth. Use 1¼" (32mm)-thick cedar if you can find it. The thicker the wood, the more depth you can get in your project. Consider laminating two pieces of ¾" (19mm) cedar if you can't find the thick wood.

- Use a ½" (13mm) shim for the wing.

- Use a rotary tool to add feather details on the tail and wing (pieces 30, 33, 34).

- The roof slopes back at the top and the left side.

- To cut out the acrylic insert, place clear tape on both sides. Use a #3 reverse-tooth blade operating at a slow speed. After, sand the edges lightly on the drum sander.

- Leave the bird seed section (13) flat so the acrylic fits over it easily.

- Spray varnish the wood pieces. Let dry overnight. CA glue the acrylic in place; make sure the glue is under the area where the bird is placed so it will be covered. Glue the bird in place. Flat sand the back of the entire piece.

- Attach two eye bolts and a chain hanger for a realistic finish touch.

Materials

- 2" x 5" x 1" (51mm x 127mm x 25mm) black wood (ebony)

- 4" x 4" x ¾" (102mm x 102mm x 19mm) medium-dark wood (dark cedar)

- 6" x 5" x ½" (152mm x 127mm x 13mm) medium-dark wood for seed (lacewood)

- 16" x 6" x 1" or 1½" (406mm x 152mm x 25mm) medium wood (cedar)

- 2" x 2" x 1" (51mm x 51mm x 25mm) white wood (poplar)

- 3" x 4" x 1" (76mm x 102mm x 25mm) yellow wood (yellowheart)

- 1" x 1" x 1" (25mm x 25mm x 25mm) orange wood (cocobolo)

LEGEND

→ Grain direction
B Black or dark shade
MD Medium-dark shade
M Medium shade
W White shade
Y Yellow shade
O Orange shade
−¼" ¼" (6mm) thinner wood
+¼" ¼" (6mm) thicker wood or riser
------ Shim

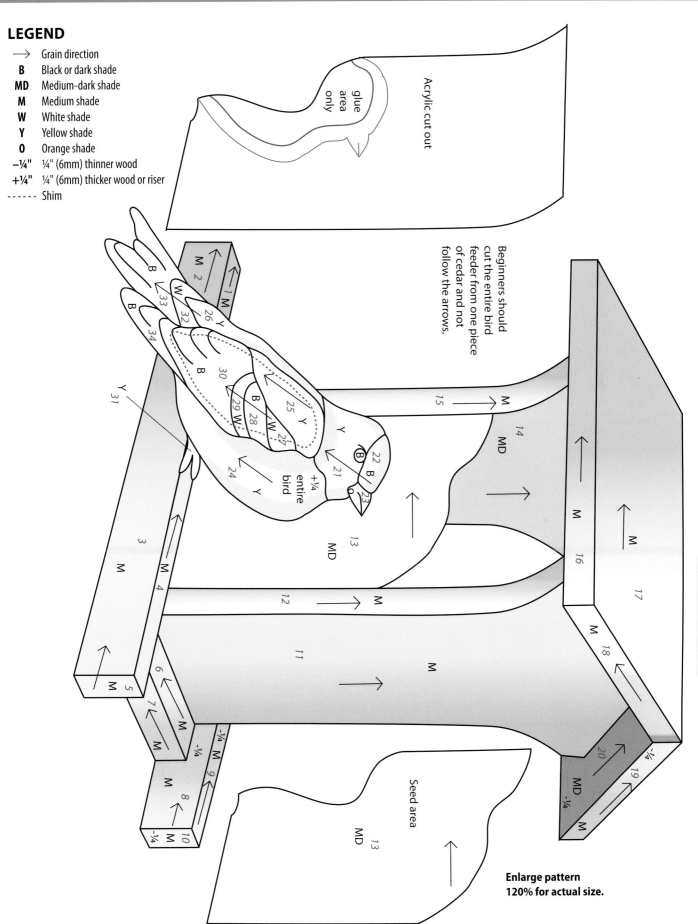

Acrylic cut out

glue area only

Beginners should cut the entire bird feeder from one piece of cedar and not follow the arrows.

entire bird

Seed area

Enlarge pattern 120% for actual size.

LEVEL 3

Boy on Swing

Materials

- 8" x 2" x 1" (203mm x 51mm x 25mm) medium-dark wood, swing (black walnut)
- 18" x 4" x ½" (457mm x 102mm x 13mm) red wood, leaves (bloodwood, dark cedar)
- 15" x 5" x 1" (381mm x 127mm x 25mm) medium wood, branch (cherry)
- 18" x 4" x ½" (457mm x 102mm x 13mm) yellow wood, leaves (yellowheart, light cedar)
- 2" x 3" x 1" (51mm x 76mm x 25mm) dark wood, shoes (wengè)
- 4" x 5" x 1" (102mm x 127mm x 25mm) medium wood, boy's pants (beech)
- 7" x 6" x 1" (178mm x 152mm x 25mm) red wood, boy's shirt (bloodwood)
- 7" x 4" x 1" (178mm x 102mm x 25mm) yellow wood, boy's hair (yellowheart)
- 7" x 5" x 1" (178mm x 127mm x 25mm) light wood, arms and neck (poplar)

Tips

Drill the holes in your swing and use a rotary tool to carve a slot for the rope to be glued into on both arms.

You can stack cut the right sets of leaves—just flip one over and it will fit in place.

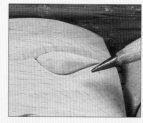

Round each of the folds of cloth. Look at this small wrinkle. Notice how it is sticking up too high. To fix this, mark and sand down until it has a nice deep valley, but rounded edges.

- Have fun with this pattern. Adapt it any way you want. It would make a great gift for a son or daughter, or even a grandchild. You can customize the color of hair and clothing. You could also make the shirt solid color or striped.

- If you are a beginner, cut the shirt from one piece of wood and the pants from another piece. This way your fitting should be easier.

- Leave the area on the arms where the rope lays bare without a backer board.

Girl on Swing

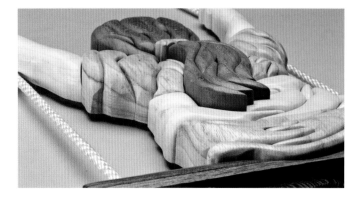

Materials

- 8" x 2" x 1" (203mm x 51mm x 25mm) medium-dark wood, swing (black walnut)
- 18" x 4" x ½" (457mm x 102mm x 13mm) red wood, leaves (bloodwood, dark cedar)
- 15" x 5" x 1" (381mm x 127mm x 25mm) medium wood, branch (cherry)
- 18" x 4" x ½" (457mm x 102mm x 13mm) yellow wood, leaves (yellowheart, light cedar)
- 5" x 4" x 1" (127mm x 102mm x 25mm) dark wood, girl's pants (wengè, black walnut)
- 7" x 4" x 1" (178mm x 102mm x 25mm) medium wood, girl's hair (cherry)
- 5" x 3" x 1" (127mm x 76mm x 25mm) white wood, girl's shirt (poplar)
- 6" x 6" x 1" (152mm x 152mm x 25mm) yellow wood, girl's shirt and scrunchie (yellowheart)
- 3" x 2" x 1" (76mm x 51mm x 25mm) dark wood, shoes (black walnut)
- 7" x 5" x 1" (178mm x 127mm x 25mm) light wood, arms and neck (poplar)

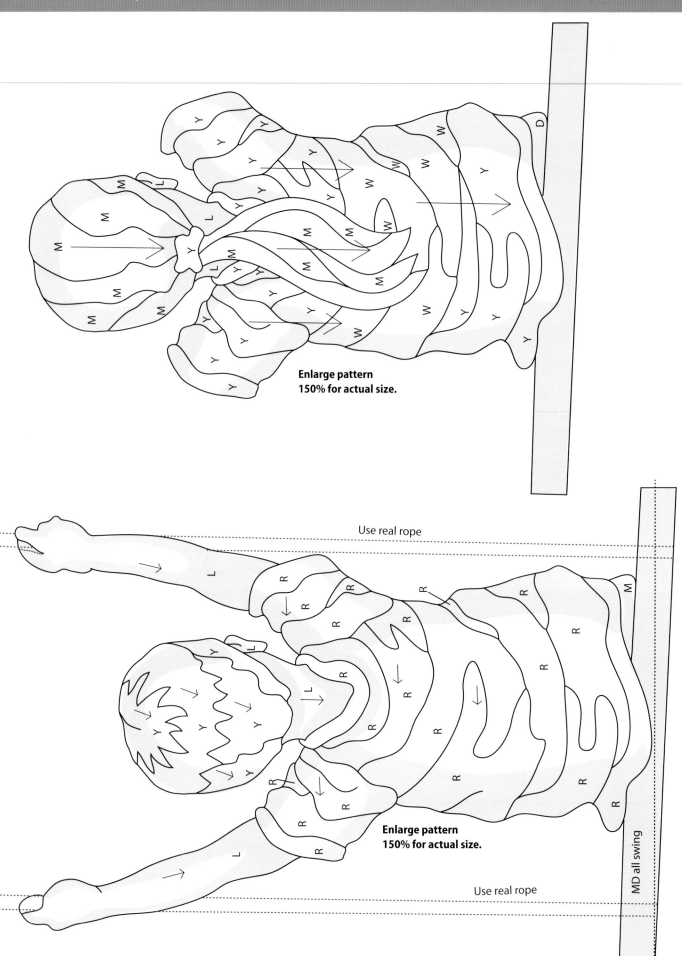

Enlarge pattern
150% for actual size.

Use real rope

Use real rope

MD all swing

Enlarge pattern
150% for actual size.

LEVEL 3

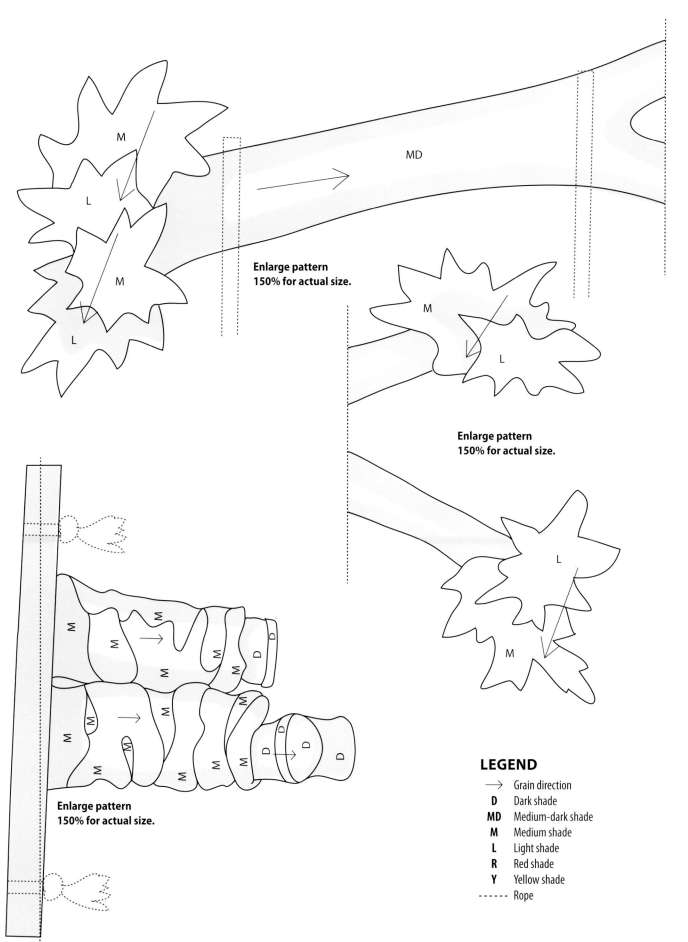

Enlarge pattern 150% for actual size.

Enlarge pattern 150% for actual size.

Enlarge pattern 150% for actual size.

LEGEND

⟶	Grain direction
D	Dark shade
MD	Medium-dark shade
M	Medium shade
L	Light shade
R	Red shade
Y	Yellow shade
- - - - -	Rope

LEVEL 3

Appendix: Exercises

EXERCISE 1:

Cutting Simple Lines and Curves

This exercise will help you to practice the cutting skills necessary for creating beautiful intarsia pieces. If you are just starting out using your scroll saw you can use this practice lesson to develop your cutting expertise.

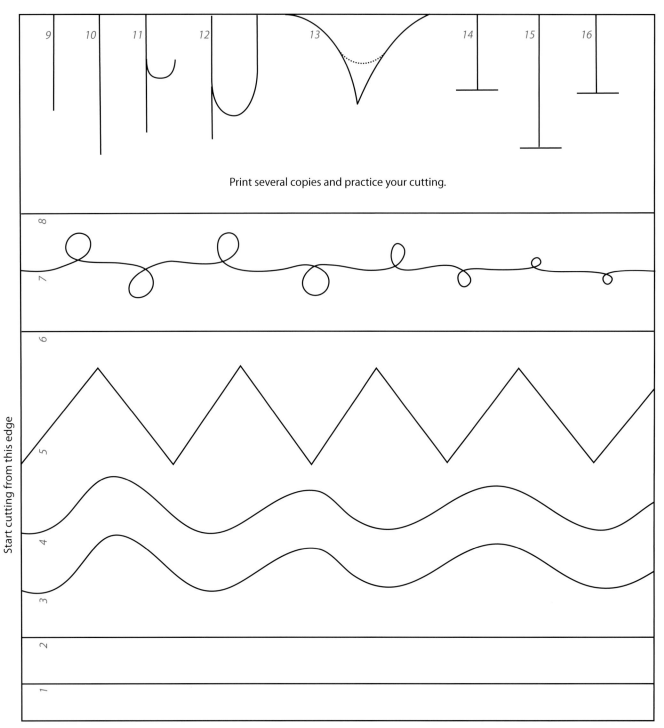

Print several copies and practice your cutting.

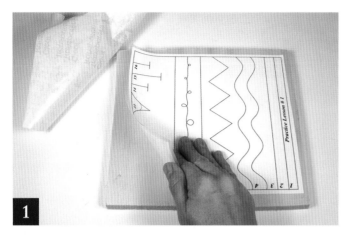

Attach pattern: Start with a 8" x 9" x ½"-thick (203mm x 229mm x 13mm-thick) piece of soft wood like cedar, popular, or pine. Use a #3 or #5 reverse-tooth blade—it will be easier to practice sharp turns with a small blade. Spray and mount the pattern.

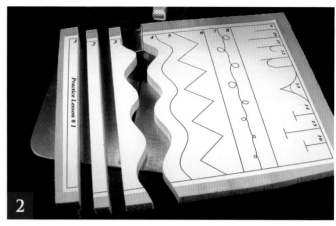

Cut straight lines: Begin with lines 1 and 2. Cut slowly and keep on the line. Lightly push the wood into the blade. Let the blade do the cutting. If you wander off the line, ease back into the line—do not back up. You may have to feed the wood into the blade at a slight angle to keep it on the straight line.

Cut curvy lines: Next, cut lines 3 and 4. Gently twist the board from side to side to keep the blade on the line. Remember, don't push from the side—steer the board so the blade stays on the line.

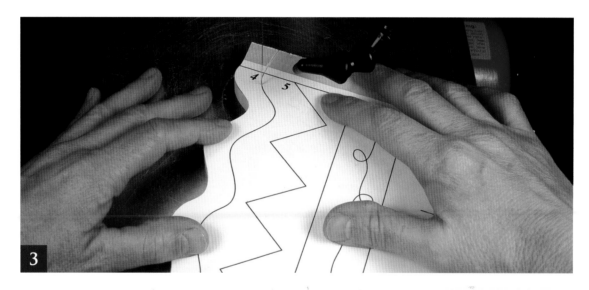

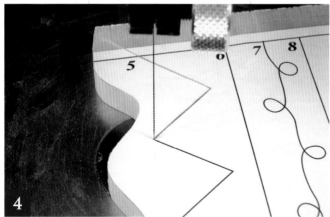

Cut sharp turns: Cut line 5. When you get to the end of the straight section, let up on the blade and move the wood very slightly forward. This moves the blade off the wood and will make it easy to turn. Twist the wood 90° so the blade is now pointed in the correct direction. Continue cutting and repeat.

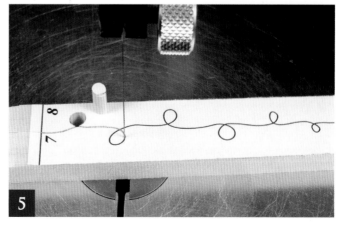

Cut loops: First, make two straight cuts (6 and 8) so you have a smaller piece of wood to handle for the next practice cut. Turn your wood completely around as you follow line 7. The loop may fall out while cutting. Stop the saw and remove the small piece so it doesn't get caught in the blade slot below. Continue making smaller and smaller loops.

6

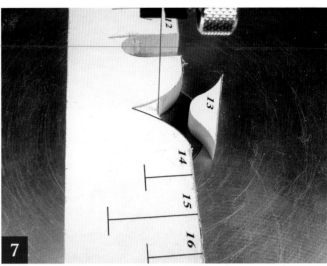

7

Cut back-up lines and curves: Cut off the top edge. Then, cut lines 9 and 10. Cut to the end of each line, then back your blade out of the cut. Next try lines 11 and 12. Cut to the end of the line, then back your blade to the curve and cut. Back out of the curve and all the way out.

Cut a sharp angle: Cut to the tip of line 13. Back up your blade to the dotted line. Cut the dotted line all the way off the end. Remove wood. Cut back to the tip from the other side, being careful not to cut deeper than the end cut.

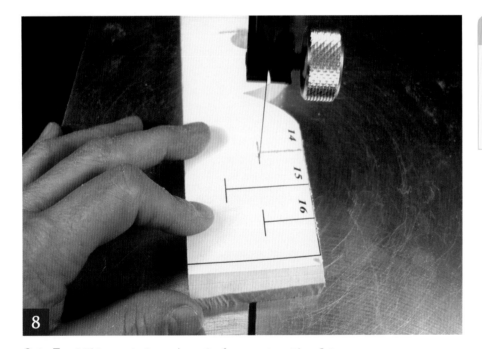

8

Cut a T cut: This exercise is good practice for accurate cutting. Cut to the end of 14, then turn the wood 90° to the left so the blade is lined up to cut the top right line of the T. Cut to the end and back out to where you turned, turn the wood 180° and cut the other side. Back out. Try it several ways until you can move the blade in your cuts without trimming more wood.

Tips

- Take your time. Do not push the wood—let the blade cut at its own speed.

- Keep practicing with this pattern until you feel comfortable.

EXERCISE 2:
Cutting Order

This segmentation LOVE project will put the practice scrolling from the last exercise to good use. This project shows how to make good choices for cutting line order.

Materials

- 11" x 9" x ¾"–1" (279mm x 229mm x 19mm–25mm) soft wood (cedar, poplar, pine)

Tips

- Cut lines in this order: red, green, blue, orange, pink, black.

- Follow the direction of the arrows for cutting.

- By cutting the green line, you eliminate the need to make sharp turns at the top of the L and one side of the V.

- The L requires a sharp pivot, as well as a back-up cut.

- After drilling the blade entry holes in O and E, sand the bottoms if there are any burrs from the drilling.

- Sand the letters and stain, paint, or varnish as you choose.

LEGEND

- ▶ Direction of cut
- ⋯⋯ Cut in waste area

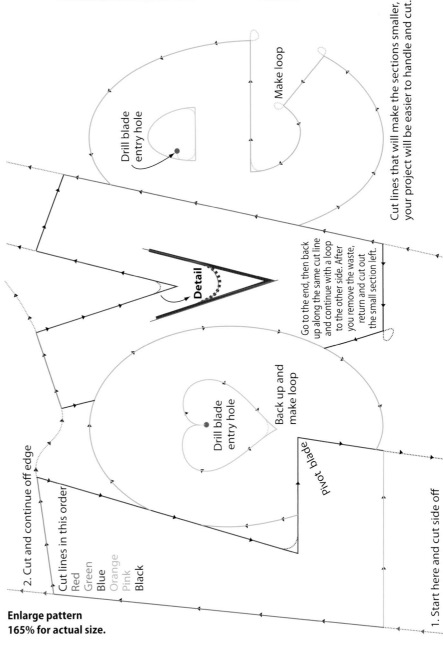

Cut lines that will make the sections smaller, your project will be easier to handle and cut.

Make loop

Drill blade entry hole

Detail

Go to the end, then back up along the same cut line and continue with a loop to the other side. After you remove the waste, return and cut out the small section left.

Back up and make loop

Drill blade entry hole

pivot blade

2. Cut and continue off edge

Cut lines in this order:
Red
Green
Blue
Orange
Pink
Black

1. Start here and cut side off

Enlarge pattern 165% for actual size.

EXERCISE 3:
Practicing the Basics

Follow the color-coded lines to cut this simple pig project from one piece of soft wood. Use the same basic steps for cutting, sanding, and gluing as described in the Goldfish step-by-step project (page 10).

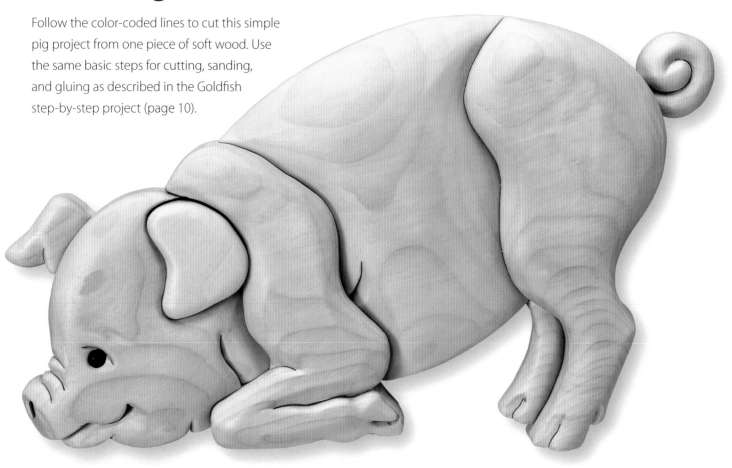

Materials

- 9" x 11" x ¾"–1" (229mm x 279mm x 19mm–25mm) soft light wood (cedar, poplar, pine)

Tips

Sand the tail and other small areas like the legs and mouth using a small Dremel or die grinder with a ½" or ¼" (13mm or 6mm) sanding band or cutting bit. You can also use a carving knife if you prefer. Clean out your cuts using the knife.

- Cut lines in this order: red, green, blue, orange, pink, black.

- Follow the direction of the arrows for cutting.

- Gently round the edges of your pig, taking off more wood in the gray areas marked on the sanding guide.

- Use pliers or forceps to hold small pieces to the sanding drum.

- Round the end of a dowel and cut to fit into the eye hole. Woodburn, stain, or paint the end. Insert into the hole and glue in place.

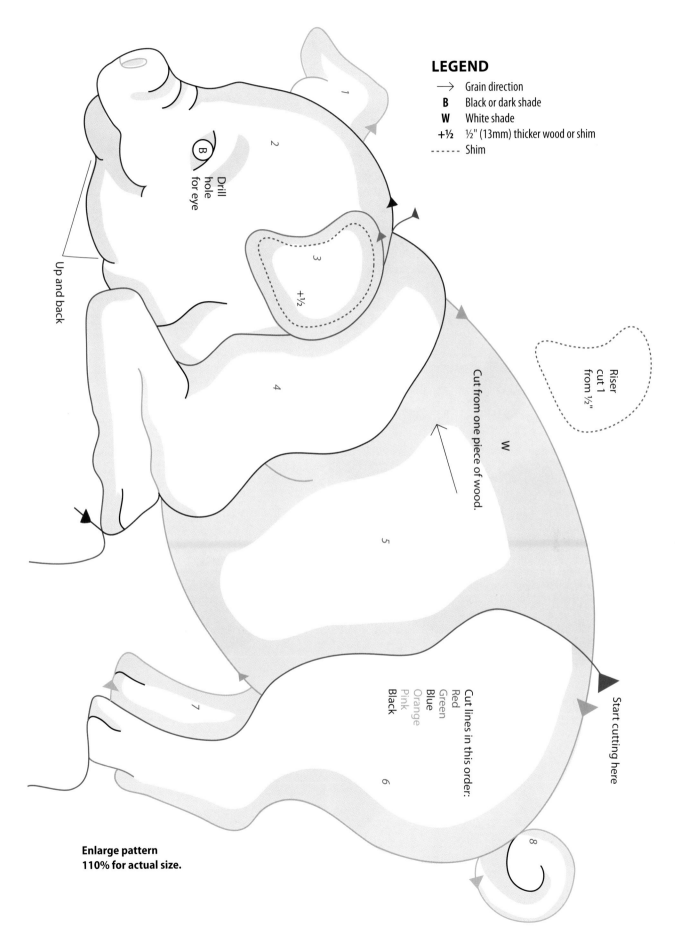

LEGEND

→ Grain direction
B Black or dark shade
W White shade
+½ ½" (13mm) thicker wood or shim
- - - - Shim

Drill hole for eye

B

Up and back

+½

Cut from one piece of wood.

W

Riser cut 1 from ½"

Cut lines in this order:
Red
Green
Blue
Orange
Pink
Black

Start cutting here

Enlarge pattern 110% for actual size.

EXERCISE 4:
Cutting for Close Fit

Multiple wood intarsia requires careful cutting to ensure that the pieces fit together. The yellow highlighted lines on this two-color panda project are the areas that need to be cut accurately for a good fit. Cut slowly and carefully to stay on your lines.

Tips

- The yellow highlighted lines on the pattern need to be cut slowly and accurately, especially the front ear and lower leg areas. Precisely cut lines will make fitting much easier.

- The area near the front ear should be lower to make the ear stand out.

- Use a carving knife or a die grinder with a burr to carve the lines of the paws and under the mouth. Sand on the sanding mop for a nice finish.

- Round the eye and nose and woodburn them to get a nice black finish. Put a clear gloss on the eye.

Materials

- 10" x 8" x ¾" (254mm x 203mm x 19mm) black wood (black walnut or wengè)
- 8" x 8" x ¾" (203mm x 203mm x 19mm) white wood (poplar)

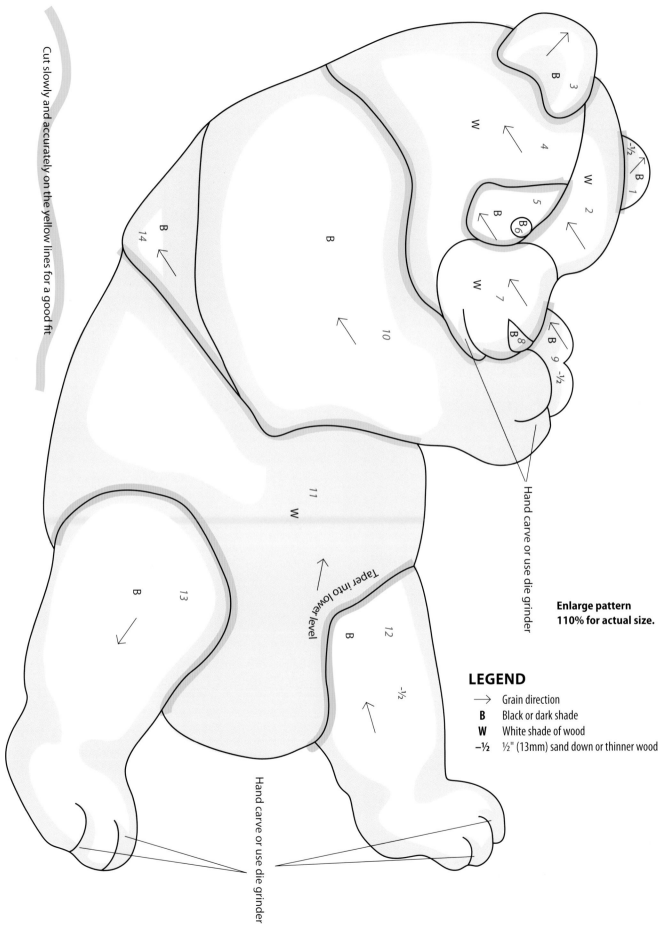

Cut slowly and accurately on the yellow lines for a good fit

Hand carve or use die grinder

Enlarge pattern 110% for actual size.

LEGEND

→ Grain direction
B Black or dark shade
W White shade of wood
−½ ½" (13mm) sand down or thinner wood

Hand carve or use die grinder

EXERCISE 5:
Recutting to Fit

Because intarsia made with more than one type of wood requires carefully fitting pieces that were originally cut apart separately, sometimes your pieces will not fit together tightly. As your skills develop, you will become better at cutting the pieces correctly the first time. However, being able to recut your lines while holding two pieces of wood together is an invaluable skill to have. Don't be discouraged if you don't get the hang of it right away, as it is a technique that needs to be practiced. Once you master the process of recutting your pieces, you will no longer have unsightly gaps in your projects or pieces that do not fit.

Cut the strips: Use a #3 or #2 skip or reverse tooth blade to cut Side A from a dark piece of wood and Side B from a light piece. Don't worry about being too exact on your lines—you'll have more gaps to fix that way.

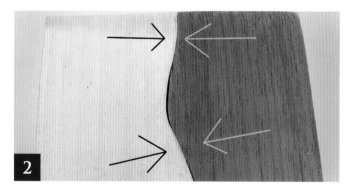

Pair and mark: Cut apart the sections where the dotted lines are on the pattern and number each one on the bottom. Pair up your numbers, starting with 1. While holding the two pieces together, put them up to the light to see where the gaps are. Mark the areas that are touching—this is where you will cut so the pieces are drawn together.

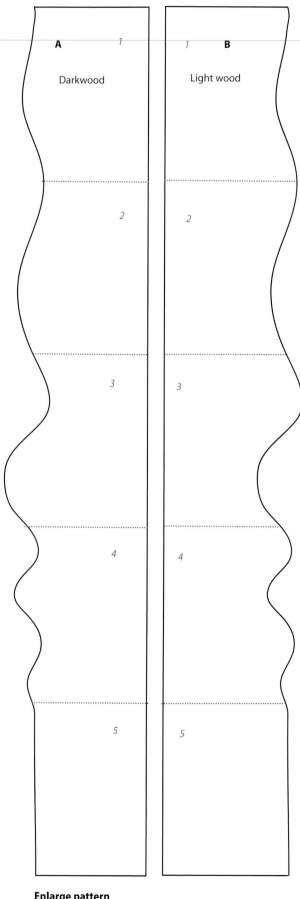

A 1   1 B

Darkwood   Light wood

2   2

3   3

4   4

5   5

Enlarge pattern 110% for actual size.

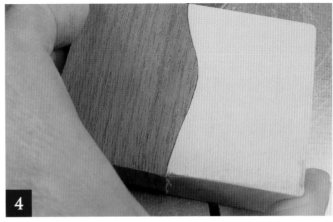

Recut 1: Hold the two pieces together and put a few pieces of clear tape across the bottom and ends. This will help hold the pieces from slipping until you get used to holding them while you cut. Cut slowly and carefully while gently pushing the two pieces together. You will feel the blade slip through the gap areas and slow down to cut at the tight areas.

Check: When you are done, hold the two pieces up to the light and check for gaps again. Repeat if you still have a gap.

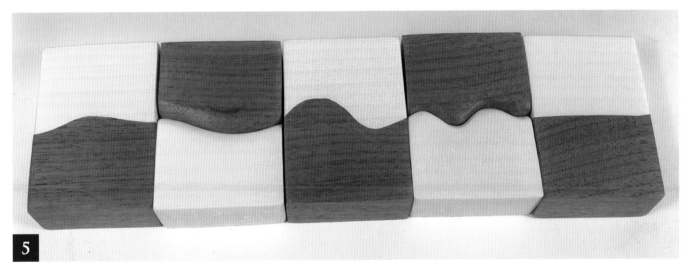

Cut 2–5: Cut out the rest of the practice patterns. Try doing a few without the tape on the bottom. When you are able to get a consistently tight fit, you are ready to use this technique on your intarsia.

Tips

- Straight lines, like practice piece 5, can sometimes be the hardest to recut. The wood can easily slip as you are cutting. Use tape to help stop the pieces from slipping.

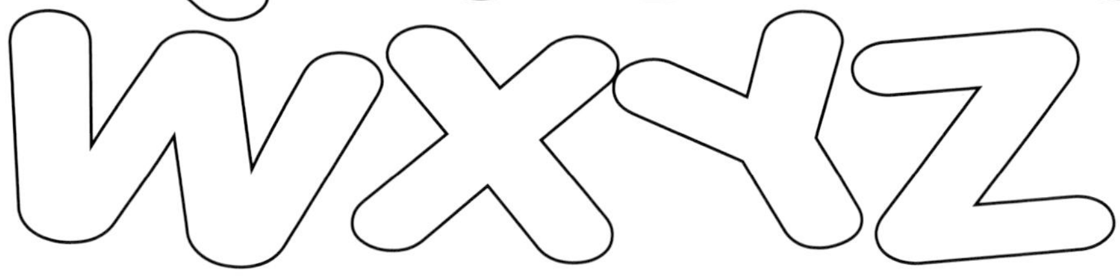

abcdefg
hijklmno
pqrstuv
wxyzABC
DEFGHIJ
KLMNOP
QRSTUV
WXYZ

Practice cutting these letters to really refine your scroll saw skills. You can also use them on the Butterfly Nameplate (page 39) and Train Photo Frame (page 70) projects.

Tool Information

You can create beautiful intarsia using only a scroll saw and a small hand sander, but having better tools will make your experience far more enjoyable and less time consuming. Buy the very best you can afford.

Scroll saw

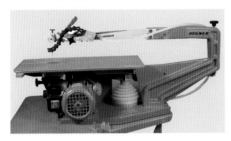

The scroll saw is a wonderful tool—with its thin blade, you can make straight, curved, and 180° turns with no difficulty. If you do not already own a scroll saw and plan on cutting large projects, pick a saw with a large throat depth and a table. Talk to local scroll saw clubs and see if you can find a few members that will let you try their saws before you buy. The Scroll Saw Association of the World (SAW) has a website that can help you contact members and local clubs: **www.saw-online.com**. Have your saw chair at a comfortable height. Check your blade to see if it is square to the table. Check your tension. Have adequate light and wear a dust mask. Cut slowly, carefully, and stay on your lines. Most of all, keep cutting as much as you can—your skill level will improve.

Band saw

From narrow ripping to re-sawing planks into thin pieces, a band saw is a versatile machine. I use it for cutting large pieces of wood into smaller more manageable pieces to cut on the scroll saw. It also works well to thin down cut intarsia

pieces to save time sanding. A rip or re-saw fence is a good investment if you buy rough sawn wood or have access to thicker stock.

Table saw

Fitted with the right blade, a heavy-duty table saw makes short work of a variety of cuts, including rips, bevels, crosscuts, miters, and compound-angle cuts. A basic fence system will aid in cutting framing for your intarsia projects or for just cutting down lumber to a smaller size.

Drill press

Whether you have a floor-standing or bench model, you will enjoy the ease of having improved control, alignment accuracy, and enhanced feed pressure over your hand-held drill. A good drill press bores holes exactly where you want them; some even have a laser guide light. Driving large bits into hard thick wood requires a lot of pressure, something a drill press does easily. Multiple speeds, keyless chucks, and adjustable tables make this a good machine to have in your woodworking shop.

Thickness planer

A planer is a must for rough-sawn wood or for making your wood thinner. You must have a flat surface on the bottom of your wood when cutting—uneven wood causes vibration on the saw and bad fitting later. You can also plane wood into ½", ¼", or ⅛" (13mm, 6mm, or 3mm) thicknesses. You can plane rough areas out and even put an almost finish-sanded surface on your wood by using the finer setting. Buy at least a 13" (330mm)-wide model.

Blades

There are two different kinds of blades for the scroll saw: pin-end, which has a small pin at the top, and the more popular plain-end. Many modern saws take plain-end blades and most older saws only accept the pin-end. Plain-end come in smaller sizes and more varieties. Here are some of the types available.

Reverse-tooth blades

Five to seven teeth at the bottom of the blade are reversed and leave a clean edge on the bottom of your piece. They produce exceptionally clean cuts in standard and premium plywood.

Skip-tooth blades

Every other tooth is eliminated, which clears dust and removes chips quickly.

Standard-tooth blades

Regular-tooth blades have teeth that all run in the same direction. They will leave a burr on the bottom of the wood. Use a #3 or smaller blade for pieces with sharp turns or small details and for soft or thin wood. Use the small blade for cutting larger sections into smaller pieces; it will have a smaller kerf and your pieces will fit better. Use #5 or #7 for harder or thicker wood and for cutting outside edges.

Dust collection system/air cleaner

For safety's sake, you should have a good dust collection system on your dust-making tools and an air cleaner for your shop. Some woods are toxic and can cause serious heath conditions. Also wear a dusk mask when you are sanding or cutting.

Pneumatic drum sander

I use my pneumatic drum sander for 95% of my sanding. Because it has an air-filled bladder inside a canvas sleeve covered by sandpaper, it will give slightly when you push against it. I use rubber fingertips to protect my fingers from being sanded. My sander has two drums.

On the bigger 8" (203mm) drum, I put 100-grit sandpaper to remove wood quickly. The other drum is 2" (51mm) and I have 180 grit on, which puts a nice finish on the pieces. It is very important to have a good dust collection system attached to your drum sander and use eye protection and a dust mask while you are sanding. Push your wood lightly into the drum when sanding. Remove

a small amount of wood at a time and place your pieces often back into your project. Learn to lightly push your wood into the drum, backing off and pushing in again as you roll.

Oscillating spindle sander

This is a great tool for adjusting and fitting pieces. It can also be used instead of a small grinder for inside curves or concave areas. I use it often for areas around eyes and other tight places. The sanding spindle moves up and down as it spins, using a dual action that sands curves smooth and fast. You can use a variety of interchangeable rubber drums that range from ¾"–3" (19mm–76mm). Sandpaper sleeves fit over the rubber drums. Nothing works better for putting a perfect 90° angle back onto pieces that were cut with a slant.

Sanding mop

A sanding mop consists of an arbor stacked with serrated sandpaper sheets and spacers that form a wheel. I think they work best mounted on a variable speed grinder, but they can be mounted on a drill press or even a hand drill. Variable speed is useful since some woods, like cherry, will burn at high rpm. I use the 120-grit mop first and then move on to the 220 or higher grit for the final finish sanding. The rougher grit will take sharp edges off the wood, which can save some sanding time. When using the sanding mop, always wear eye protection and a dust mask. Hold your pieces lightly against the mop. Keep your wood moving or you will wear down

your piece too much in one area. If you push too deeply into the mop or don't have a good hold on your piece, the mop will send it sailing to the floor. For small or hard to hold pieces, I use forceps or needle nose pliers.

Flat drum sander

A flat drum sander has a flat surface with a rotating drum located in a slot in the middle. I have a 12" (305mm) sander that works great for large or small pieces.

It works well to clean and flatten the bottoms of cut pieces and to remove any glue that may be left on the bottoms of the pieces when I glue them together. It will also nicely flatten any uneven wood pieces or remove burrs from regular skip tooth blades.

Small rotary tools

Small micro air die grinders or variable speed electric rotary tools work best for sanding small areas, inside curves, or carving accents. For inside or hard-to-reach edges I use a grinding burr.

Carving tools

On some projects you may have to do light carving. If you are unfamiliar with carving knives, a good investment would be a basic carving book. A few good-quality carving knives are wonderful to have on hand. An X-Acto knife with a new blade can be a workable alternative. Have a sharpening stone handy to keep a good edge to your blade. Use caution with the sharp knives and purchase a protective carving glove to use. Watch the amount of pressure you use and make sure if your knife slips there is nothing in the way to cut accidentally. Woodworking and carving are inherently dangerous—enjoy your craft, but keep safety foremost in your mind whenever you are in the shop.

Woodburner

Try using a woodburner to add small details to your intarsia quickly and easily (see Cowboy Boot Clock, page xx). Some areas, such as an eye on a small project, can be burned in rather than cut (See Cat, page xx). Invest in a good quality woodburning unit that has adjustable temperatures and assorted tips.

Other useful tools and supplies:

Clamps and/or sand bags

Router & bits

Finishing sander

Circular saw

Needle nose pliers/forceps

Sandpaper

Gel/spray varnish

Dust mask

Clear contact paper

Spray adhesive

Double-stick carpet tape

Clear packing tape

Glue stick

CA glue and solvent

Index

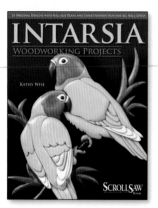

Intarsia Woodworking Projects

21 Original Designs with Full-Size Plans and Expert Instruction for All Skill Levels
By Kathy Wise

From a celebrated intarsia artist comes 21 original full-size patterns. Included are step-by-step tutorials.

ISBN: 978-1-56523-339-3
$19.95 • 80 Pages

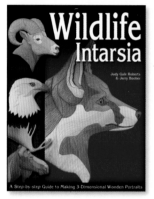

Wildlife Intarsia

A Step-by-Step Guide to Making 3-Dimensional Wooden Portraits
By Judy Gale Roberts and Jerry Booher

Learn to create beautiful wood inlay art for North American wildlife, including a wild mustang, a bull moose, and a bald eagle. Includes tips for simulating fur, and all of the basics for getting started.

ISBN: 978-1-56523-282-2
$19.95 • 128 Pages

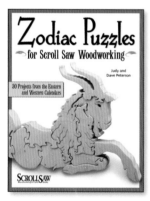

Zodiac Puzzles for Scroll Saw Woodworking

30 Projects from the Eastern and Western Calendars
By Judy and Dave Peterson

Crafters will find inspiration in the stars with this collection of scroll saw patterns based on the astrological signs of the Western and Chinese zodiacs.

ISBN: 978-1-56523-393-5
$17.95 • 96 Pages

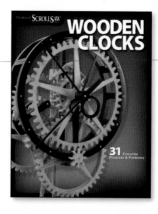

Best of Scroll Saw Woodworking & Crafts: Wooden Clocks

31 Favorite Projects & Patterns
By Editors of *Scroll Saw Woodworking & Crafts*

The most beloved clock projects from the pages of Scroll Saw Woodworking & Crafts. Includes grandfather clocks, pendulum clocks, desk clocks, and more.

ISBN: 978-1-56523-427-7
$24.95 • 152 Pages

Wooden Bowls from the Scroll Saw

28 Useful and Surprisingly Easy-to-Make Projects
By Carole Rothman

You will not believe these bowls were made without a lathe! Includes 28 easy-to-make projects for crafting beautiful bowls with a scroll saw.

ISBN: 978-1-56523-433-8
$19.95 • 136 Pages

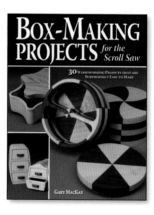

Box-Making Projects for the Scroll Saw

30 Woodworking Projects that are Surprisingly Easy to Make
By Gary MacKay

Now woodworkers of any skill level will be able to easily make their own decorative and functional boxes. 30 beautiful and easy-to-make boxes to show-off your scrolling talents.

ISBN: 978-1-56523-294-5
$17.95 • 144 Pages

SCROLLSAW
Woodworking & Crafts

In addition to being a leading source of woodworking books and DVDs, Fox Chapel also publishes *Scroll Saw Woodworking & Crafts*. Released quarterly, it delivers premium projects, expert tips and techniques from today's finest woodworking artists, and in-depth information about the latest tools, equipment, and materials.

Subscribe Today!
Scroll Saw Woodworking & Crafts: **888-840-8590**
www.FoxChapelPublishing.com